W9-BVR-581

The Education of an Archbishop

BOOKS BY PAUL WILKES

These Priests Stay
Trying Out the Dream: A Year in the Life of An American
   Family
Six American Families
Merton: By Those Who Knew Him Best
In Mysterious Ways: The Death and Life of a Parish Priest
Companions Along the Way

For Children
Fitzgo, the Wild Dog of Central Park
My Book of Bedtime Prayers

The Education of an Archbishop

Travels with Rembert Weakland

Paul Wilkes

ORBIS BOOKS

Maryknoll, New York 10545

The Catholic Foreign Mission Society of America (Maryknoll) recruits and trains people for overseas missionary service. Through Orbis Books, Maryknoll aims to foster the international dialogue that is essential to mission. The books published, however, reflect the opinions of their authors and are not meant to represent the official position of the society.

Copyright © 1992 by Paul Wilkes

Published by Orbis Books, Maryknoll, NY 10545

Much of this book appeared originally in *The New Yorker* as "Profiles: The Education of an Archbishop," in the summer of 1991

Manufactured in the United States of America

Library of Congress Cataloging-in-Publication Data

Wilkes, Paul, 1938-
    The education of an archbishop : travels with Rembert Weakland / Paul Wilkes.
        p. cm.
    "Appeared originally in the New Yorker as 'Profiles: the education of an archbishop,' in the summer of 1991"—T.p. verso.
    ISBN 0-88344-836-X
    1. Weakland, Rembert. 2. Catholic Church—United States—Bishops— Biography. I. Title.
BX4705.W385W55 1992
282'.092—dc20
    [B]   92-17246
                                                                              CIP

Contents

v

❧{ **INTRODUCTION** }❧

I first met Archbishop Weakland in the early 1980s when I was preparing a documentary on Thomas Merton for public television. Weakland had been in Bangkok when Merton died — of an accidental electrocution — and had officiated at the memorial service there.

Over the next ten years I followed Weakland's career both as the archbishop of a moderately large American city (where I, coincidentally, had gone to college) and as a church leader who was becoming nationally known. His work on the Catholic bishops' pastoral letter on the economy, and his "listening sessions" with women on the issues of birth control and abortion, had made him one of the more recognizable members of the American Catholic hierarchy.

Although members of the hierarchy have been written about before, I felt that an in-depth profile about a man with Weakland's wealth of experience, depth of intelligence, and obvious candor could provide some insights into an occupation and lifestyle that both Catholics and non-Catholics find rather mystifying.

When I first approached the Archbishop with the idea of writing about him, I asked if he would allow me not only to have extensive conversations with him, but to accompany him in his daily work—whatever that work involved. I said such an approach would provide the fullest picture possible. He agreed and imposed no ground rules.

As I began to spend time with the archbishop, I quickly realized that this was more than a single article. As my notes and research grew, I knew that I wanted to write at a greater length in order to tell in detail about Weakland: at work in Milwaukee, at a national bishops' meeting, and finally on a trip to war-torn El Salvador. But I also felt the archbishop's story offered an opportunity to consider the role of the hierarchy in American Catholicism and to show how the Vatican deals with its appointed leaders.

What follows is that look—much longer than I had planned—into the life of a Roman Catholic archbishop. The period covered is about three months.

Throughout the time I spent with Archbishop Weakland—and, as I continued my research and interviewing in the months that followed—I found him a rather extraordinary subject, given his ecclesiastical position. Not once did he say something was "off the record"; he allowed me complete access to all his meetings, functions, and ceremonies. He answered all my questions straightforwardly.

If the pages that follow are at all successful in depicting the life, work, and thoughts of an American prelate, it is because this particular archbishop believed in what he was doing and that—with God's continued help—he had nothing to hide.

PART I

❧{ **MILWAUKEE** }❧

I n the Archbishop of Milwaukee's mail on a Monday morning in September after his return from a month-long vacation were communications from Dr. Adrian Holderegger, a senior professor of the Faculty of Theology at the University of Fribourg, in Switzerland; Archbishop Agostino Cacciavillan, the newly appointed Apostolic pro-nuncio, or Vatican Ambassador, to the United States; and Briana Ziolkowski, a first grader at St. Philip Neri elementary school, on Milwaukee's North Side. And there was the latest sheaf of letters from the self-styled Little Eucharistic Lamb, a parishioner in her early forties. The Archbishop was addressed variously as "Excellency" (by Professor Holderegger), "Archbishop Weakland" (by Archbishop Cacciavillan), "Uncle Rembert" (by Ms. Ziolkowski), and "Most Reverend Archbishop Weakland" (by the Lamb). Although still suffering from jet lag after his trip—a visit to Siberia, Poland, and the Ukraine—Archbishop Rembert George Weakland, O.S.B., was also energized, from having seen firsthand a Catholic Church emerging from the oppression of recently defunct Communist regimes. He found himself eager to resume work in his own archdiocese, where he is the spiritual leader of more than six hundred thousand Catholics.

On reading part of Professor Holderegger's letter—

"You will receive the *doctor honoris causa* on the occasion of the celebration of the hundred years of the Faculty, at the date of the 15th November, 1990. In the meantime, we expect the consent of Rome" — the Archbishop smiled a bit boyishly, as he is wont to do when he is praised or congratulated. He would have to check flight schedules before he could reply; the date fell at the end of the annual meeting of the National Conference of Catholic Bishops, in Washington, and just before a planned trip with three of his fellow-bishops to El Salvador. Switzerland was hardly en route. "Fribourg, Fribourg," he said pensively, tapping his lower lip with his index finger and turning in his chair. "Their theology school is run by Dominicans," he said. "Much of the encyclical *Rerum Novarum* originated at that university, a hundred years ago. I can recall a classroom there with a plaque commemorating all that work, which rather boldly laid the foundation for Catholic social thought. I gave a talk at Fribourg once. I imagine they think I have something to do with that whole area of the Church's teaching — making sure it lives on, that is."

He went back to his mail, and took up the letter from the nuncio. The smile slowly mutated into an expression of wry amusement, as though someone had confronted him on the street and requested something outrageous framed in a perfectly reasonable argument. Archbishop Cacciavillan's letter concerned "a published report that a Religious Sister has been appointed to the office of Academic Dean of Saint Francis Seminary in Milwaukee," and observed that "such an appointment would be a matter of concern" to the Congregation for Catholic Education, in Rome. Dictating his response to his administrative assistant, Delphine Meyer, Weakland said that he had just returned from vacation, and needed to consult the seminary's rector before answering formally, but in his last paragraph he noted with the slightest flicker of ecclesiastical snappishness that "the Rector of our Seminary was previously the Director of the Office of the National Conference of Catholic Bishops for Priestly Formation, and I am sure he is well aware of any legislation that exists on this matter."

"Oh, it's just a lob into my court, Del," the Archbishop said, as Ms. Meyer awaited his next letter. His tone was even; the smile was back. "Very Vatican of him. Wants to know what my case is without indicating his own. So I just lobbed it back." He opened a large manila envelope from Ms. Ziolkowski and carefully unfolded a poster-size piece of construction paper divided into twelve panels, one of them proclaiming "Happy Birthday, St. John the Baptiser," another depicting stalks of wheat interspersed with succulent-looking bright-green weeds. The Archbishop had asked Milwaukee Catholic grade-school children to illustrate either the feast days that fell on summer Sundays or the Scripture passages from those Masses; there were to be winners in three categories, and their prize was to be dinner with the Archbishop, after which he would play the piano for them. "Have to find a competent judge for these," he said to Ms. Meyer, adding Briana's work to a stack of other submissions. "And, as for the Little Lamb, it's time. She claims that she's possessed and that only I can exorcise her. She's having visions, revelations. She's a saint, doing penance for others. Problem is, she has a few priests believing her. I've got to get a panel of three or four psychologists together and have them interview her. It's turning into a cult. This has to stop."

Rembert George Weakland is one of three hundred and five bishops and archbishops appointed to the hundred and eighty-eight dioceses and archdioceses of the Roman Catholic Church in America. His morning's mail is a fair sample of what a Catholic prelate of his rank encounters. The honorary degree would be his sixteenth; it was an acknowledgment of the esteem in which Weakland is held in some quarters of the Catholic Church for his forthright yet measured stands on many of the social and doctrinal issues with which the Church is beset. The letter from the nuncio was the latest round in a continuing *mano a mano* with the Vatican, which has not been so ready in its praise, and to which an outspoken man like Archbishop Weakland is somewhat suspect. Briana represents the youngest of the many populations he attempts to serve, and the Eucharistic Lamb the ardent, impassioned fringe of Catholic belief.

While Weakland is, by Church fiat and tradition, the autonomous leader of things Catholic within the forty-eight hundred square miles of his archdiocese — a domain embracing two hundred and eighty-seven parishes and missions, five colleges and universities, a hundred and sixty-eight elementary and high schools, twelve hospitals, nine hundred and fifty-three priests, a hundred and two brothers, twenty-eight hundred nuns, and thousands of deacons and lay workers — he finds himself in something of a marginal position these days. For all those who applaud and honor him, there are many who want him deposed, censured, or silenced. He is, moreover, one of a decreasing number of prelates appointed before 1978, when the current Pope, John Paul II, was elected; more than half the American bishops now holding office have been appointed since that time. If one characteristic links these newer members of the hierarchy, it is that they are far more comfortable with the doctrinal orthodoxy that John Paul II espouses than with the more open and pastoral spirit of his recent predecessors — one of whom, Pope Paul VI, appointed Weakland an archbishop in 1977.

His minority status within the American hierarchy aside, Weakland is something of an anomaly among Catholic bishops. He is not a product of the diocesan priesthood, which produces the vast majority of the episcopate; indeed, he never served as a parish priest. He is a Benedictine monk: Rembert is his monastic name, and the O.S.B. stands for Order of Saint Benedict. Belying the image of monastic life as one spent within the cloister, he has travelled extensively since he was ordained, forty years ago, and he is fluent not only in Latin and Italian — the lingua francas of Catholicism — but also in German, French, Portuguese, Spanish, and Russian. He is a concert-quality pianist, having trained at Juilliard. For some twenty-eight years, he has been a religious superior: first as a Benedictine abbot, then as the abbot primate for the Benedictine order worldwide, a post he held for ten years before he became an archbishop. His staying power is noteworthy. Becoming a bishop or an archbishop is no longer universally considered the splendid capstone to a clerical career; for some it is closer to a millstone.

American bishops complain openly and often that they are being pulled in two directions at once. A significant proportion of their constituency neither pays them homage nor looks to them for guidance yet demands that they work to bring about change in the Church's stand on issues ranging from priestly celibacy and the ordination of women to birth control and abortion. At the opposite pole are the traditionalists, who implore them to return the Church to the certainty it enjoyed before the Second Vatican Council, and are ready to report perceived transgressions to Rome. Even some of the new appointees find themselves chafing under the mantle of dogmatic consistency the Vatican wants them to wear. It is an extraordinary period in the life of the American Church—one that Church historians see as more dissonant, in terms of the disparity between the beliefs and practices of the faithful and the official teaching of the Church, than ever before. It is a time when the unimaginable happens regularly. In recent years, several bishops have resigned their posts because of alcoholism, scandal, or simply the stresses attendant on the office. The stress factor alone has been enough to cause a number to take extended leaves of absence: Archbishop Raymond Hunthausen, of Seattle, who was censured by Rome for incorporating women, former priests, and homosexuals more fully into the workings of the Church and for allowing non-Catholics and divorced Catholics to receive Communion, is perhaps the best known of these; others are Archbishop John Quinn, of San Francisco, and Bishop Eugene Gerber, of Wichita. The *National Catholic Reporter* noted in a major article last year that American bishops now freely admit that the stressful nature of their posts "is taking a severe toll on their physical and mental health." And yet Archbishop Weakland, though he is at the vortex of the Church's *Sturm und Drang*, not only carries the burden of his office easily but plainly enjoys what he does for a living. Unlike many of his brother bishops, he seems to have dealt successfully with his personal shortcomings and professional frustrations. He has avoided being typecast either as a categorical liberal, like Thomas Gumbleton, of Detroit, and Francis Murphy, of Baltimore, or as a diehard conservative, like Austin Vaughan, of New York, or Theodore McCarrick, of Newark. If he is not the most vocal or the most widely recognized bishop in America, he is probably one of the most effective.

The job — if it may be called that — of bishops is defined by canon law: they are "teachers of doctrine, priests of sacred worship, and ministers of governance." They are also "successors of the Apostles by divine institution"; in no other religion is there both a line of consecration going back to the founder (in this case, Jesus Christ) and a codified global hierarchical system ultimately responsible to one person (the Pope). As members of an episcopate that was firmly established by the early second century, Catholic bishops are at once the supreme authority within their sees and the linchpins linking their people and priests to the Vatican — the place where Church doctrine is forged and safeguarded. Canon law further states that a bishop possesses all power "required for the exercise of his pastoral office, except for those cases which the law or a decree of the Supreme Pontiff reserves to the supreme authority of the Church or to some other ecclesiastical authority." Some canon-law experts interpret this to mean that there is no actual restriction on the power of a bishop: the only limitations are his willingness and his ability to wield that power. A bishop's power is termed "ordinary" — that is, inherent in the office — and although the Pope can curb the exercise of episcopal power or delimit the geographical area in which it is exercised, he cannot alter or suppress its essential character. In practice, however, it is autonomy on a leash—a leash whose length each prelate must determine for himself, and which can be tugged at any time by the hand of Rome.

A rchbishop Weakland is a tall man, about six feet two, with thinning brown hair and a slight paunch that nudges his black clerical shirt over his belt. He is sixty-four years old. His eyes are hooded by fleshy lids, which give him a somewhat grandfatherly appearance. His lips are thin and have a tendency to purse before and between sentences. The drama inherent in his office is cloaked in a steadfast routine, and on my first visit to Milwaukee late in the summer, when he was living in the rectory of the Cathedral of St. John the Evangelist (he has since moved into a renovated brick house on the grounds of the archdiocesan seminary), his meticulousness was apparent. The apartment, a suite of three rooms on the rectory's second floor, was neat and airy, lined with shelves holding records and compact disks (mostly classi-cal, and arranged alphabetically by composer) and books (so many that his library long ago overflowed into nearby guest rooms). His living room was dominated by a Mason & Hamlin grand piano, its surface kept bare, out of a craftsman's pride in the fine tool of his trade; within the solid wood case and steel frame, built in 1912, was a new, German-made movement. In an adjoining study was a reclining chair with a stack of books on the floor beside it, among them a Russian edition of *The Brothers Kara-*

11

mazov, works on the Middle East by David Shipler and David Grossman, some Italian novels with the English translation on facing pages, and Iris Murdoch's *Message to the Planet*. On the desk was a laptop computer, on which the Archbishop writes position papers, pastoral letters, a weekly column for the *Catholic Herald* (the archdiocesan newspaper), and reviews for publications ranging from the New York *Times* to *Commonweal*.

His day began, the Archbishop told me, with a period of "puttsing and praying." He would awaken around six, and, being a slow riser, shuffle about in bathrobe and slippers "half praying, half daydreaming." He might sit in what he referred to as a "yogish" position for a period of meditation, or spend fifteen minutes exercising on a NordicTrack beside his bed. After a shower and shave, he would read the Scripture passages for the morning's Mass, and then take from his closet one of eight identical black suits and a pair from among ten pairs of black lace-up shoes. (Although his wardrobe also includes slacks, sports shirts, and innumerable sweaters — the bane of most priests and bishops, because they receive so many as presents — he has no nonclerical suits and owns only one sports jacket.) On most mornings, he would descend to the rectory's common room at seven-fifteen and join the two priests of St. John's — Father James Brady and Father James Lobacz — and his priest-secretary, Father Leonard Van Vlaenderen, for morning prayer. Then he would walk through a series of passageways to the cathedral, where he customarily said the seven-forty-five Mass, unassisted by an altar boy or a lay reader. Much like parish priests throughout America, he would turn on the lights himself, refill the cruets with water and wine, take hosts from an airtight jar, light the altar candles, and vest in the sacristy. Only when he reached into a drawer and withdrew a purple zucchetto, the silk skullcap that is the sign of his office, was it apparent that he was not simply a priest.

Some fifty people regularly attended the seven-forty-five Mass, at which the Archbishop would deliver a four- or five-minute homily. Often the theme dealt with the vicissitudes of belonging to a changing Church and the need for faith in the midst of it all. "The Pharisees make me nervous—washing the outside of the cup, then the inside of the cup—so wrapped up in the incidentals," he told his congregants one morning. "We all have to be on guard to see what is really important. Me, too. When I'm confirming a girl with so much blow-dried hair over her forehead that my thumb has to fight its way through the thicket, am I thinking of that incidental or the power of the sacrament? Is it against our faith to allow girls to assist at the altar, or is that just an incidental? We get so provincial, so worked up about such silly things, and we forget what really counts."

After breakfast, at which the Archbishop would read through three newspapers—the Milwaukee *Sentinel*, the Chicago *Tribune*, and the New York *Times*—Father Van Vlaenderen would drive him, in an episcopally appropriate dark-red 1988 Pontiac Bonneville, to the chancery, some ten minutes away in the Archbishop Cousins Catholic Center, on South Lake Drive. Weakland passed his driver's test years ago, just before leaving for a conference of Benedictine abbots in Rome, but his first forays behind the wheel in the Eternal City terrified him. He has a Wisconsin driver's license, but he prefers not to exercise this temporal privilege.

Weakland's chancery office is sparer than the study in the rectory, and much larger. Here his bookshelves hold a set of the writings of the Church Fathers, the code of canon law, and a set of *Origins*, a weekly publication of the Catholic News Service containing the latest Church documents along with reprints of speeches and reports affecting the Church. Space is not at a premium in the Center, a sprawling pale-red-brick complex built by Weakland's immediate predecessor, William Cousins, who had intended it as a preparatory seminary. It was finished in 1963, just as the bottom was about to drop out of priestly vocations with the upheavals following Vatican II, and was meant to accommodate five hundred students. In 1979, when Weakland shut it down, only a hundred and fifty were enrolled. The building was turned into archdiocesan offices and a retirement home for priests in 1984, and it may well be the only Church administration building in America with a full-sized swimming pool and a basketball court of such quality that it is used for practice by a National Basketball Association team, in this case, the Milwaukee Bucks.

Archbishop Weakland usually reserves the morning for attending to administrative tasks, reading and answering his correspondence, and scanning his airmailed copy of *L'Osservatore Romano* and items from the Catholic News Service wire which have been highlighted for him by the chancery's Communications Office. Over his desk is the official photograph of the one man on the face of the earth to whom he is accountable—Pope John Paul II. The Pope's is a steady, powerful gaze, at once immediate and eternal, riveted on the opposite wall. Behind the Archbishop, on a table, is a two-foot-high bronze sculpture of

Pope Paul VI, the man who appointed him. Paul's head is cocked quizzically, his arms are extended, and his eyes are trained squarely on the middle of Archbishop Weakland's back. It is difficult to imagine a sound—except, perhaps, the bark of a drill sergeant—emanating from the strong, bold picture of the current Pope. But from the sculpture might come a far less commanding voice—that of a fellow-foot soldier who knows well the vagaries of battle.

Though Archbishop Weakland handles an enormous amount of paperwork, he is hardly an executive centrist. He delegates routinely, and he has a cabinet, made up of both clergy and laypeople, to which he has given broad powers within the archdiocese. It is a point of pride with him that he can leave for a month, as he did on his recent trip, and never have to phone the office.

Often, the Archbishop has lunch in the chancery cafeteria, sitting with a different group of archdiocesan employees—there are some two hundred people on the staff—each day. The afternoon typically holds a full schedule of appointments and staff meetings. The range of people Weakland sees is impressive, both in its variety and in its size; many of his visitors could well have their concerns dealt with at a less exalted level. A C.E.O. whose conglomerate has an annual budget approaching a quarter of a billion dollars—the total of chancery, school, and parish expenditures in Milwaukee—would certainly be more discriminating. The Archbishop's appointment calendar is the antithesis of management by objective. One afternoon, a Nigerian priest currently serving in a Chicago parish was accorded a hearing even though the Archbishop knew full well that the man would be asking for personal financial aid (some of which the archdiocese of Chicago was already providing) and also for help for his diocese back in Africa (a function more properly left to the Society for the Propagation of the Faith or to a mission office within the diocese). Nonetheless, Weakland listened graciously to his pleas for more than twenty minutes, and told him what channels he might make use of. Next came a delegation of angry laypeople, who complained about the way priests were being assigned to parishes; they wanted more say in the matter. The archdiocesan vocation directors expressed doubts about a new approach to recruitment; the president of a Catholic women's college wanted to know whether she should ask for the resignation of a board member who was about to proclaim his pro-choice stand on abortion (Weakland said he didn't think it was necessary but would support her decision); members of Milwaukee's Hmong community asked him to attend their upcoming national convention.

The next morning, a delegation of six Milwaukee Ukrainians came to see the Archbishop. They were disturbed by a lecture he had given at their church in which he alluded to the historical anti-Semitism of Catholics in Ukraine. Weakland invited the group to lunch (Milwaukee bratwurst and a pot of baked beans), and the conversation elucidated his manner of "dialogue"—a word often used in religious circles these days. Quietly and with great dignity, and always addressing him as "Your Excellency," the Ukrainians—four men and two women—called the reports of pogroms by Ukrainian Catholics during the Second World War blatant lies. The conflicts with Jews were over "political differences" or were due to "economic pressures," they said, and were not acts of anti-Semitism. They

spoke in defense of John Demjanjuk, a Ukrainian con-
demned to death by an Israeli court for atrocities committed at Treblinka. How could they teach their children
pride in their Ukrainian heritage, they asked, when such
slurs abounded? The Archbishop listened attentively,
and—as is his custom in emotionally charged situations—
responded circuitously. Instead of addressing their points
directly, he reviewed the highlights of his recent trip to
their homeland. "There was Archbishop Sterniuk—who
spent decades in a tiny room in Lvov, not allowed to say
a public Mass—finally in the cathedral, which had just
been returned to use as a Catholic church, with thousands
of people around him, all of them weeping with joy. I stood
beside him, and was honored to take Communion from
his hand." The Milwaukee group nodded approvingly, for
(as Weakland knew) the eighty-five-year-old Volodymyr
Sterniuk is a figure beloved by Ukrainians all over the
world.

"It is a wonderful time for Ukrainian churches," Weakland continued. "But, yes, what you read in the papers is
true. Anti-Semitism is on the rise. In Ukraine, in Russia,
in Poland. I saw anti-Semitic signs in Krakow, and I asked
the tour guide why they weren't painted over, and she said,
'Oh, it's nothing.' Not only there but here. In Kenosha, in
Madison—worldwide. I mentioned this issue to Archbishop Sterniuk." Weakland paused for effect, and they
nodded sombrely, waiting for the judgment of a man they
trusted. "And he agreed. It's with us again, and we have
to be watchful not to let it go on."

The Ukrainians thanked the Archbishop profusely for
affording them a hearing, and before they left they asked
to have their picture taken with him.

"What I didn't say to them," he told me later, "was that although Sterniuk acknowledged the rise of anti-Semitism, he also remarked, 'Oh, you know how they' — meaning Jewish people — 'are.' And when I asked him if he shouldn't say something about anti-Semitism he countered with 'Oh, no. Then we will have to admit we were wrong.' How would it help things if I told these good people about that, just so I could win the argument? That's easy to do, but what's gained by it? I didn't live Sterniuk's life. I don't know what pressures he's under. It's easy to come in for a few days and know exactly what everybody should do and say; we bishops have a talent for that. I think that now they'll be a little more sensitive about the issue of anti-Semitism. That's all you can do. Nothing changes dramatically. Life is a series of almost imperceptible changes. You hope you're moving people in more or less the right direction.

"Are some of these meetings boring? Unnecessary? A waste of time? People need to talk, to be heard, even though nothing will come of it, and" — he smiled — "I need to listen, though nothing may come of it. I often think I know exactly what needs to be done, but I'm terribly wrong sometimes. I need to speak both to those who are my friends and to those who are not my friends. But in real dialogue. If you want to exercise any meaningful authority in the Church today, you have to listen not just to the most agreeable voices, and not solely to the edicts of Rome. Rather, you listen to where the spirit is — you hear one small voice, and you say, 'That's it!' Not consensus — that's no way to lead. I'm surely influenced by the third chapter of the Rule of St. Benedict: When anything important is brewing, you call the community together and listen for the spirit. And you allow the youngest, least experienced member to speak first, so he won't be overwhelmed by all the experts."

Archbishop Weakland always makes room for members of one group: like all Catholic prelates today, he finds himself spending a considerable amount of time dealing with his priests. Vocations are shrinking precipitously – in Milwaukee as well as in virtually every diocese in the United States. In 1977, when the Archbishop was appointed, he had five hundred and forty-seven diocesan priests available to serve two hundred and sixty-five parishes. Today, he has only three hundred and seventy-four active parish priests, but four additional parishes. It is not only a matter of trying to fill vacancies with an ever-decreasing number of available and competent men (whose average age is greater by six years than it was when Weakland arrived); the priests themselves now demand more attention. Most of them are stretched to the limit: some priests cover two or three churches, and some are forced to preside at four, five, or six Masses on Saturdays and Sundays. Weddings, baptisms, funerals, hospital visits blur into each other as one long day melts into another. The Archbishop will quickly see any priest who asks for an appointment, but unless there is a troublesome situation or a pressing need he rarely instigates such a meeting. "They give far too much weight to a call or a personal letter from me," he commented after a phone call from one beleaguered priest. "It's usually only a case of my wanting to talk something out. So a long time ago I stopped asking them to come in."

When his office day is finished, usually at 4:30, it is a rare day that Father Van Vlaenderen will take the Archbishop back to the cathedral rectory to spend a leisurely evening. More often, the work of the Archbishop goes on. On one fall afternoon, he was standing at 4:45 in the fifth floor dining room of the University Club, overlooking Lake Michigan, sipping a dry sherry before a meeting of the Archdiocesan Education Foundation. The existence of the group signals the predicament of financing Catholic education at a time when the legions of religious men and women who once staffed them at negligible pay have dwindled; and the Archbishop wants to evince his interest and render, with his presence, his support. Yet there is another, more subtle statement being made as the archbishop and this group of Catholic lawyers, bank executives, and top-level managers exchange small talk. When I was an undergraduate at Milwaukee's Marquette University in the late 1950s, the only Catholics who entered this club wore white jackets, not dark, served cocktails and did not partake of them. J. Michael Bolger, a campus leader whom I remembered from those Marquette days, now the president of this lay group, had gone on to become a very successful Milwaukee lawyer and was about to take over as president of Medical College of Wisconsin, a huge medical complex. Catholics are now part of Milwaukee's power elite, and Weakland stood shoulder to shoulder with them on the beachhead they have finally secured. Steak au jus was served at the 5:30 dinner meeting that followed and, Milwaukee being a family kind of town, these executives could be home not long after 7:00.

Catholic education is increasingly expensive and difficult to sustain and nowhere is the situation more critical—and more vexing—than in Milwaukee's central city, which during my visits was experiencing a spate of violent crimes that would eventually result in a new yearly record being set for the number of murders. And so, on another evening the archbishop drank a can of beer and dined on fried chicken and soda biscuits in the basement of Holy Angels Church on North 12th Street near Capitol Drive, squarely in the middle of a declining black and Hispanic neighborhood. There he met with a handful of white priests — among the few who will still accept this kind of assignment — and the black and Hispanic parents and teachers who know that the church's presence, and the school's existence, are crucial to the area's fragile grip on stability.

One beachhead secured; another, precariously holding on. Here, in the kind of neighborhood where the bulk of the city's Catholics once lived — and where the church was once the center of their lives — families are now under the merciless bombardment of poverty and drugs and violence. Both beachheads are strategic high ground, both in the care and on the conscience of the spiritual father of Milwaukee's Catholics.

As I spent my days in Milwaukee watching the Archbishop function both as an executive in the office and as the Church's representative at groundbreakings, installations, and the myriad other events he attends, I found him to be a strange amalgam. At once painstaking in his search for the right course, he could treat seemingly consequential matters with alarming dispatch; sometimes the humble servant, he had flashes of shameless pride; he was the competent, supremely confident executive and the lost, helpless boy. When a manuscript for a high-school course on moral issues on which his imprimatur was requested crossed his desk, he took no more than ten minutes to read parts of it before attesting to its doctrinal correctness, having assigned the line-by-line reading to a monsignor whose judgment he respected. After listening deferentially to a string of visitors, he somewhat self-consciously deplored his indecision about which of his honorary-doctorate cowls to wear to a local ceremony. (The answer proved as self-conscious as the dilemma: "I'll wear my *ferraiola*" — the scarlet floor-length cape of his office — "instead. That will outshine them all. Other bishops love to wear theirs on public occasions like this.") He can unflinchingly make the difficult decision to remove an ineffective pastor or to spend hundreds of thousands of dollars on a construction project, yet he has not mastered the simple sequence of numbers required to make a long-distance call on the chancery telephone system. He refuses to drive. There is acuity in decision making, a certain reluctance to fully grow up, the controlled arrogance of an intelligent man — controlled most of the time.

"Like almost everybody else, I'm a swirling mass of competencies and insecurities," he said one afternoon, allowing me a brief glance into a box that is usually well sealed. "When I feel I'm over my head, I become officious, moody, mechanistic. It's then that I say to myself, 'Is anybody going to listen to a poor kid from Patton, Pennsylvania? Will they find out who this is beneath the fancy robes?' Everyone who thinks Weakland is always so sure of himself should live in Weakland's head for a while."

Patton is a town of twenty-two hundred inhabitants, high in the bituminous-coal region of the Allegheny Mountains of western Pennsylvania. George Weakland was born there, in 1927, the youngest son of Basil and Mary Weakland. There were two older sisters and an older brother; two more sisters would follow. Despite the fact that Patton was the headquarters for the area coal companies and was made up of a broader cross-section of people than most Pennsylvania mining towns are, it was a remote, windswept outpost. Basil Weakland, having served in the Marine Corps during the First World War, followed his father into the management of the family-owned Palmer House, a four-story local hotel with a wrap-around porch, where the family lived. A fire gutted the hotel in 1929. "It killed my father, too," the Archbishop recalls. "Somehow, there had never been enough to challenge him in that little town. After the fire, he never really worked again—just sat in the charred rooms day after day, depressed. During the War, he had served in the Dominican Republic, and he probably picked up malaria there; a few years after the fire, he developed pneumonia. But my mother was very wise about it: she didn't shield us from the fact that he was dying. We were in the room when he died. I remember the death rattle.

He had a military funeral, and I also remember, very well, taps being sounded, and the second bugle answering from the distance. His actual funeral Mass I have no memory of."

At their father's death, the oldest Weakland child was nine, the youngest seven months; George Weakland was six years old. His mother, who had been a grade-school teacher before her children were born, was forced onto public assistance in the ensuing years, and the family faced the indignities of poverty. "Down on rent," they moved from one shabby house to another, and Mary Weakland made meal after meal of the surplus corn meal, powdered eggs, and milk they were allotted. Still vivid in the Archbishop's mind are the Sunday mornings, when his mother sought to predict which Mass the better families, who had paid for the pews on which their names were emblazoned, would attend. On too many Sundays, she guessed wrong, and the Weaklands would be sent to the rear of the church when the rightful occupiers appeared.

But along with the indignities of being poor, there was a strength running through the family. Mary Weakland was a proud woman, who bore her circumstances with a certain grace and presented herself for welfare food or clothing as if she were shopping at a fine store. Just to be a Weakland was to bear an old and revered name in the largely immigrant coal range: the family had arrived in America around 1641. Family folklore included stories of intermarriage with Indians, of the hardships of the American frontier, of the struggle to keep a Catholic faith alive without the benefit of clergy; back when Weaklands first settled in Pennsylvania, baptisms were performed and marriages witnessed by Catholic elders. It was a family that had overcome adversity before.

George plunged into books well before his schoolmates learned to read. By the age of seven, he had taught himself to pick out tunes on the family's upright piano. At eight, he began to work his way through a ten-volume set of Elson's "World's Best Music," and completed much of it before he had his first piano lesson. ("What else was there to do in a small Pennsylvania town when you had no money and few toys?" the Archbishop remarked.) By the time he reached the seventh grade, he was playing the piano more than respectably, and the next year he was made a church organist. The top student in his small, four-room grade school, he quickly became accustomed to being singled out for excellence. His mother used to have to shoo him out of the house so that he would get some air; George was more interested in music and the workings of his mind than in games of mumblety-peg, catch, and hide-and-seek. If the early pictures of him in the family photograph album are any indication, he was happy in his self-made world; he appears perpetually on the verge of bursting into laughter.

Nevertheless, as the Archbishop and I walked the streets of Patton one bitterly cold winter afternoon and he pointed out the landmarks of his youth I got the impression that he was talking about a boy who was to him something of an artifact, a period piece. He had once been that boy, but along the way some tie had been broken — a necessary severing, as it turned out.

Like many a good Catholic boy of that time, young George played priest. His sisters bought Necco wafers, which he used as hosts, and served as the members of his congregation while he offered "Mass." Their dolls filled in as the faithful departed when he officiated at funerals, with candles from the kitchen and appropriate weeping from his sisters. But George went beyond being merely a good little boy: he ascended to that higher form of youthful Catholic behavior that makes a certain type of nun swoon and gives other children the irresistible urge to put spiders down your back. Georgie Weakland was a "scroop"—one of those fervent Catholic kids who not only scrupulously obey the letter of the Church's law but seek ways to confront the irresolute and lead them to virtue. One Thursday night, his mother returned from working in the kitchen at Patton's Fraternal Order of Eagles and announced that she had brought home some leftover chicken salad, which would do nicely for Friday-night supper. George declared that he would not partake of it. The fact that there was no icebox in the house and the chicken salad would spoil meant nothing to him; eating meat on Friday was an outright mortal sin. George rallied his siblings to boycott the meal, and then bragged about it to the other altar boys at the Church of Our Lady of Perpetual Help. He was overheard by Father Bertrand McFadyen, the local pastor. Father McFadyen was decidedly unimpressed. "There is a divine law, and there is human law," he said sternly to George. "This is a case of human law. Now, you go home and eat that chicken salad."

While George was still in grade school, Father McFadyen took him and a few other altar boys to visit the Benedictine Archabbey of St. Vincent, in Latrobe, some sixty miles away, where McFadyen himself had studied for the priesthood. Back in Patton, George had his family, the upright piano, the parish church, and two eighth-grade sweethearts, but when he saw St. Vincent's he truly fell in love. Founded in 1846, it was the oldest Benedictine community in the country. He was awed by its imposing double quadrangle, built in stark Bavarian monastic style, where the monks spent their days at once apart from the world and enfolded in community life. He walked the hallways, with their fine wood wainscoting and vaulted ceilings; he knelt in the magnificent church, amid towering pillars, each a solid piece of granite from Scotland. There was a huge library, and there were seemingly countless pianos; music issued from the church and from practice rooms. Men walked about in black habits, black scapulars flowing from their shoulders in front and in back, symbolizing the Christ they had taken on as their protector and advocate. Most of the men seemed happy to have given up the pleasures of the world, of marriage and family; and, indeed, to young George the experience of the monastery marked not an end but a beginning.

At the age of thirteen, he entered St. Vincent's Preparatory School. There were classes in Greek, Latin, and German; hours of practice at the piano and organ; and hours spent in the silence of the crypt below the church with his arms extended, in the emotional pleas to God of a boy intoxicated with the religious life. His musical talents blossomed, and he came to see his future as teaching music within the monastery, its seminary, the school, and the college that the Benedictines maintained. At the age of nineteen, he took his first vows as a Benedictine monk. There were then over two hundred monks at the abbey, and the more popular names were already assigned, so George Weakland was given the name Rembert, after a somewhat obscure ninth-century German saint — a Benedictine who, as it happened, was later asked to leave the cloister and become a bishop. Throughout his years as a young monk, he waited for a moment of transcendence, when he would feel the call, or hear God whisper his name. No such moment arrived, but the excitement of the place, and the fundamental goodness of the men around him, continually reaffirmed his conviction that he was in the right place. Here were God, a family, and his beloved music. Unlike many who have entered religious life at an early age, he was never to experience a major crisis of faith.

His education within the Benedictine order was amazingly diverse, and his rise through the ranks rapid. At twenty-one, he went to Rome, to study at the Benedictine college at Sant'Anselmo. He was ordained in 1951, at twenty-four—the earliest age at which a man could be made a priest without a papal dispensation. The following year, he studied music at Juilliard, and a year later also enrolled at Columbia University to work toward his doctorate.

Father Sebastian Moore, a Benedictine from England, who teaches at Boston College, was also a student at Sant'Anselmo in the late forties. He recalls the twenty-one-year-old Weakland as "a terribly good boy—you know, one of those," and continues, "He was quite conservative—perhaps too much of a fanatic for my taste. And he had that quiet arrogance about him, the self-assurance of a person who knows that he can do something very, very well—music, in his case—and that you can't. He was never considered one of the boys, and he certainly was not a monastic jock. A bit of a loner, really. I was rebelling against any authority I could find, but you could count on Rembert to be solidly on the side of whatever the Church proclaimed, regardless of what he believed in his heart.

One day, we had just listened to a beautiful piece of music, and I said, 'Can't you see, Rembert, great art like that has to be directly inspired by God.' He was aghast: 'Sebastian, don't talk that way! You'll get flunked for it.' "

While Father Rembert may have been a conventional priest, he was developing into a remarkable pianist. But if there had been any lingering thought in his mind that he would have been better off pursuing a professional career in music it was banished one night in 1948, at St. Vincent's. There, with the full Westmoreland County Community Orchestra behind him, he gave a brilliant rendition of Rachmaninoff's Second Piano Concerto. He returned to the dressing room, the thunder of applause still resounding in his ears, and it hit him squarely. "I was positively drained," he recalls. "And I knew then that I could never live like that. I could not do that, night after night." He taught music at St. Vincent's, served as the monastery's principal organist, and was eventually named head of the Music Department. Such monastery jobs usually lead nowhere; it is the theologians, philosophers, and canonists who are more likely to move on to higher office. So when, at the remarkably early age of thirty-six, he was elected archabbot of St. Vincent's it was a surprise both to Weakland and to his community.

The next few years marked a period of intense building at St. Vincent's. The community had experienced two major fires: one of them engulfed a good portion of the monastic quadrangle in flames; the other was the smoldering heat of Vatican II, which occasioned a difficult reassessment of monastic life around the world. Weakland seized the opportunity for change, entering quickly into the spirit of the Council even as other monasteries were taking their time about it. St. Vincent's priests and lay brothers were incorporated into a single egalitarian community, and the Divine Office—formerly recited by the priests in Latin, in which the brothers were not versed—was said together, in English. The younger monks were freed from their isolation and assigned to teach or work at the college, to give them more exposure to the secular world. A new residence was built, combining monastic serenity with a modern airiness and light. St. Vincent's had not established any new monasteries since the turn of the century; four were founded under Abbot Weakland, who took seriously the missionary thrust of Vatican II. Father Campion Gavaler, a contemporary of Weakland's, recalled the period as we talked at St. Vincent's one evening. "Sometimes Rembert could ride roughshod over people," he said. "But he had balls. He made the tough decisions, and he listened to the youngest novice as intently as he would to the Pope. There was no artifice about him."

In 1967, when Weakland was forty years old, all the Benedictine abbots met at Sant'Anselmo to pick a new abbot primate for their order. The office of primate carries little actual power, since each abbey is essentially autonomous, and abbots jealously protect their prerogatives. The two most recent primates had treated the position largely as a ceremonial one. Weakland had been happy running St. Vincent's and did not want the office, but after a series of ballots sentiment swung to him.

Whatever personal triumph the new primate felt faded quickly as, one by one, the abbots left for their home monasteries and he was shown to his new quarters, a spacious apartment-and-office suite on the Aventine Hill, with

French doors and a balcony looking west to the Tyrrhenian Sea. He walked about the rooms, his footfalls echoing on the polished parquet floors, and was overcome with the most profound feeling of loneliness he had ever experienced: his days of community life were over. Never a man to wallow in self-pity, he declared the next day a day off, gathered up the eight Benedictine brothers on the Sant'Anselmo staff, and went for a picnic along the Tyrrhenian. Heedless of his predecessors' example, he at once set out to become an activist leader of the Benedictines, and travelled extensively — to Africa, South America, Asia, and to monasteries in troubled areas like Vietnam and Eastern Europe. He was heartened by Benedictine vitality; he was appalled at monasteries that had deteriorated. Some monasteries, like those behind the Iron Curtain, had been virtually abandoned. "Our monastery at Pannonhalma, in Hungary, had not had a visit from a primate since 1935," he told me. "It was more an old-age home than a monastery by the time of my visit, in 1968. The monks there had taken in old men from other orders. All the religious orders were being suppressed by the government. Many of the men in Pannonhalma had not been heard from in years; no one at their various headquarters knew who had survived. I passed from bed to bed. Men were crying. One old Jesuit begged me to tell Father Arrupe, the Jesuit superior general, when I got back to Rome that he was still alive." In Africa and Asia, he encouraged small, isolated monasteries to gather in regional conferences, in order to pool their human and material resources. He saw more than simple physical privation: some neglected monasteries of Benedictine nuns in Italy had become virtual snake pits, with mentally troubled women raging in the cloister. Weakland saw to it that the sickest nuns were removed to a clinic, and that professional help was brought in to attend to the rest. And everywhere he went he introduced Vatican II reforms, sometimes to monasteries whose occupants were living as Benedictines had lived in the Middle Ages.

Some admired Weakland's organizational decisiveness and openness to change; others thought that he had too much of a penchant for siding with the minority in any debate. The Church was transforming itself at a breakneck pace, and Weakland seemed a man exhilarated by the opportunities for positive change. "Something had happened to the old boy," Father Moore recalled. "I remember a cocktail party in London in 1968, around the time the Vatican was set to issue the document reaffirming the Church's stand against artificial means of birth control. Rembert and I were talking about one of our classmates, who had been quite a radical in our day, opposed to just about everything the Pope did or said, and who had done a flip-flop and was now supporting Rome on this issue. Rembert leaned over to me and said, 'What's up with the guy? Gone completely square, hasn't he?' He was not the good little boy I'd known in the forties. He was relaxed, and he was funny."

What had happened, apparently, was that Rembert Weakland had grown up. "I was used to being Number One, and I had to prove that over and over again," he told me one night while we were having supper in Milwaukee. "The little boy from Patton, with the torn knickers, the little boy with a towering ego, had to show them—whoever 'they' were—that he was just as smart, just as quick. My smugness, my braggadocio were signs that I wasn't so sure of myself—that I felt I was in over my head, inadequate. But I found out at Juilliard, and later at Columbia, that I could do advanced academic work as well as anybody; I wasn't a monastic hothouse plant. Then, as abbot and as primate, I saw that I could handle people well. I didn't have to fall back on Church rules to make things happen; I could use my own common sense. But watch me. When I get moody and distant, it's still there—the fear that I'm not up to the job facing me. I'd like to believe that that feeling of inadequacy is behind me, but I'm still trying to prove myself."

Weakland had met the future Pope Paul VI when he was still Giovanni Battista Montini, Archbishop of Milan. In 1956, the young Benedictine had come to Milan to examine some original manuscripts of Ambrosian chant, which was his Columbia thesis subject. (The thesis, analyzing the origins of Ambrosian chant, which preceded the now more popular Gregorian chant and flourished with it for a time, made it as far as a first draft. The Archbishop claims that he could complete it in three months, if only he had three months to devote to it.) Montini immediately took a liking to the tall, scholarly priest-musician. In 1977, when the post of archbishop of Milwaukee—a city that Weakland barely knew, having visited it only a few times— fell vacant, Pope Paul appointed him, perhaps because of personal affection for him, which had deepened during Weakland's time as primate, or perhaps because he wanted to appease those members of the Curia who thought the American Benedictine too thorough a reformer of monastic life.

Before travelling to Milwaukee, Weakland was interviewed in Rome by a reporter for the Religious News Service. His statements were both forthright and, in the light of his later concerns, prophetic. He advocated a much wider role for women in the Church, maintained that the American Church had to work harder to influence American foreign and domestic policy, and argued that the Church in developing nations needed personal as well as financial support from the American Church. In Milwaukee, the news of Weakland's appointment was extremely well received. Some churchmen speculated that Milwaukee was a stepping stone: that he had a good chance of going on to a place in the Curia, or to a larger see—like Chicago, to which two Milwaukee archbishops had ascended, eventually becoming cardinals. Some went as far as to say that he might become the first American Pope.

Despite the welcome there, Weakland's early days in Milwaukee marked the lowest point in his clerical life. His predecessor, Archbishop Cousins, had occupied a handsome residence in the Milwaukee suburb of Brookfield. Perhaps it had suited Cousins' needs—he avoided close relationships in his see, preferring the company of friends in Chicago—but Weakland found Brookfield extraordinarily lonely. "There were no sidewalks," he said of his first neighborhood in the archdiocese. "Big yards, a lovely place to raise kids. I just didn't happen to have any. And wherever you went, you had to drive. I had said yes to the appointment with my lips but not with my heart. I thought it was the worst decision I had ever made." He found himself watching more and more television, running up huge telephone bills calling old friends, and finding any excuse to get out of the house to pay an evening parish visit. To the people of Milwaukee he was the energetic, friendly new archbishop; in his own mind he was an isolated, friendless man, stripped of the last vestiges of the Benedictine life he had known for thirty-seven years. He missed the excitement of Rome, the steady stream of visitors from around the world, and his own travels. His journeys as primate had taken him to Uganda, Brazil, Kuala Lumpur; now it was Kenosha, Menomonee Falls, and Waukesha. Veal saltimbocca and spaghetti alla puttanesca gave way to the beers and brats for which Milwaukee is infamous. Weakland never unpacked more than the bare essentials in the Brookfield house. Not long after he moved in, he directed that it be sold, repacked the essentials, and moved downtown to St. John's rectory.

The new archbishop knew nothing of diocesan affairs and management, never having been a diocesan priest. Moreover, he was completely unaware of the weight his words carried, now that he was the spiritual leader of a moderately large city. His offhand remarks—firmly held convictions wrapped in a thin layer of humor, harmless among monks who were sworn to each other for life—at times returned to haunt him. After just a year in office, he signalled that his romance with the new Pope was over, describing John Paul II as a "ham actor" whose pronouncements "do not always make sense, unless you dramatize them." The Pope, he said, was "very Polish and very stubborn," and "when he's made up his mind, keep quiet!" Milwaukee, of course, has a large Polish community, and local Polish leaders were incensed, accusing Weakland of ethnic insensitivity. (Weakland invited them to the chancery and played a complete tape recording of his remarks, which had also included ample praise of the Pontiff, and the storm soon passed.) Later, as pedophilia among priests was drawing increased attention, he was quoted as saying that not all victims of sexual abuse are unwitting innocents. But his gaffes, while major, were outweighed by his performance. He adroitly instituted change in archdiocesan affairs, placing women in senior positions, streamlining the bureaucracy, assuring pensions for lay employees and higher pay for teachers, establishing a program of spiritual renewal for parishes, and mandating that each parish have a lay council. He bore witness to his concern for social justice by having dinner with the city's poor and with ex-priests and their wives, by providing sanctuary for Salvadoran refugees, by protesting police brutality against blacks, by calling for civil rights for homosexuals, and by instituting post-abortion counselling. His activities soon began to attract national attention, and Milwaukee's innovative policies became boilerplate for other dioceses. (If American Catholics could vote on sainthood, the one administrative change that would likely earn Weakland this honor was his combining of the invariable Sunday "second collections" into semiannual appeals by mail.)

Along the way, he made some serious enemies among the New Right, and many of them are still working hard for his removal. There were also those in Milwaukee who found his decisive nature tactless and unfeeling. When he was reorganizing the archdiocese, he called his staff together just before Christmas and told them with great enthusiasm how wonderfully the new system would work — this despite the fact that the reorganization would cost some of them their jobs. "He doesn't have much patience with the weaker brethren," one veteran Milwaukee priest says, and a younger priest told me that among his group Weakland is referred to as the Black Hole, explaining,

"You can sit in his office and pour out the information, and it just goes in—you never know what he's thinking. And we've all heard how he was sent all over—Rome, New York—to be trained. Are there no Milwaukee priests who deserve the same opportunities? Among the hundreds and hundreds of us, is there only one brilliant Rembert?" Weakland is nevertheless enormously popular among his priests; a recent survey revealed that he has a ninety-percent acceptance rate among them.

After a rocky start, the former primate found that the running of an archdiocese could be at once interesting and substantially delegated. He developed friends, among both the priests and the laypeople of Milwaukee, and a cultural life that includes the Milwaukee Symphony and Chicago's Lyric Opera. He discovered a certain natural rhythm to his prayer life—often a silent hesitation before a meeting or conference or liturgical function, when, articulated or not, the message sent heavenward is: What do You want of this? He grew into his role, and found that his life need not be limited by the geographical confines of his diocese, or his mind enclosed by the dogmatic boundaries set in Rome.

While so much about Weakland is on the public record and, as a senior member of the American Catholic hierarchy, unusually forthcoming, another glimpse into his inner self was afforded one evening when we attended a performance of Tchaikovsky's opera *Eugen Onegin* at the Lyric in Chicago. As he summarized the libretto, he explained the role of the steadfast and earnest Lenski, who would lose the affection of his fiancée—as well as his life—to the rakish Onegin. "Oh, the good guy gets killed in a dual, but you really don't care about it. His love lacked spontaneity; that's why he was killed. It's Onegin you care about; Onegin!" And so, in the battle between the dependably good and the not-always-so-upstanding, what matters, for Weakland, is the velocity of love.

While most of his callers and their concerns are local, it is not uncommon for the Archbishop to receive national and international figures, who come to talk — and often to disagree with him — about broader issues. Such a meeting took place in June of 1984, when a draft of the pastoral letter entitled "Economic Justice for All," of which Archbishop Weakland was the principal architect, had barely begun to circulate. The letter had been commissioned by the National Conference of Catholic Bishops, and examined the impact of Catholic social teaching on the American economic system and how that system, in turn, influences the way Catholics live their lives and express their faith. The draft drew the ire not only of the Reagan-era free-marketeers outside the Church but also of a broad spectrum of Catholics, because of its call for government intervention to reduce economic disparities, for a general "preferential option for the poor," and for greater funding of welfare programs, job training, and education. The letter took pains not to castigate the capitalist system, and it was based on a nearly hundred-year-old tradition of papal encyclicals on social justice, but the Catholic audience is no longer made up only of immigrants and blue-collar workers eager to have their burden eased. Increasingly, it consists of members of the middle and upper classes, who fear that their hard-won affluence will be diminished if the less fortunate in their midst are to be helped.

"I looked out the window," the Archbishop said, remembering the day that the group of influential neoconservative Catholics was scheduled to arrive, "and up pulled these limousines with smoked windows, having whisked the occupants in from their private planes, which had landed minutes before at the Milwaukee airport. All I could think of was that it looked very much like a meeting of high-level Mafia leaders." His visitors — including the industrialist J. Peter Grace, former Treasury Secretary William Simon, and Michael Novak, a senior analyst at a conservative think tank — filed into his office, ready to launch a preemptive strike before the draft could circulate any farther. They were ushered by the Archbishop into his adjoining conference room. While Weakland can be a patient listener for that "one small voice," and a fool for Christ, he is not simply a fool. "I sat not at the end of the table, where I customarily do, but on the side, with my back to the wall — a wall covered with pictures of me with each of the Popes of recent times, and with famous churchmen like Karl Rahner, Dom Helder Camara, and Cardinals Suenens, Willebrands, and Hume," he recalled. "I wanted these loyal sons of the Church to see some of the people I've hung out with. I listened patiently to their side, and granted that I might be called a socialist for what I was saying. And then I tried to give them my view that the Church has to insert itself in the national debate or else risk finding itself declared — properly — irrelevant. Vatican II clearly restated that the free-market economy is not the be-all and end-all. And the preferential option for the poor is Scripturally based. The problem is that the preferential option has been around for so long that we have stopped looking at it. Why? Because our religion has become a civil religion, instead of the prophetic faith that calls out not for rugged individualism but for us to share what we have. As gently as I could, I said that there would be a cost to upsetting our civil religion. That we could believe in capitalism and yet be critical of its excesses. That paying attention to the common good does not necessarily mean lapsing into collectivism, Communism — those scary words."

The pastoral letter on the economy was overwhelmingly approved at the 1986 N.C.C.B. meeting, and provided Archbishop Weakland with his first national exposure. He went to Wall Street and advised a group of four hundred brokers and investment bankers to "look at the bad effects of the system, and how those human costs can be minimized or reduced, if not done away with." He addressed the Joint Economic Committee of Congress, saying that "economic policies cannot be left solely to technicians, special-interest groups, and market forces" but that government must intervene, to provide "full employment — the foundation of a just economy." The N.C.C.B. letter is cited extensively throughout the Church — in catechetical materials, speeches, and homilies — and also by those (Catholics and non-Catholics alike) who want to lend a moral or Biblical dimension to their testimony on economic issues before congressional or state-legislature committees. Pope John Paul II's recent encyclical, *Centesimus Annus* (issued to commemorate the centennial of *Rerum Novarum*, Pope Leo XIII's disquisition on the fundamental rights of labor in a free-enterprise system), also takes up the subject of capitalism, extolling its virtues but warning against its abuses; the bishops' pastoral letter is deemed to be not only more complete in its analysis of thorny economic issues but more Scriptural and pastoral in spirit.

Occasionally in our conversations, the Archbishop referred to his differences with the Vatican during his years in Milwaukee, speaking of these episodes not as examples of his courage under fire but as burdens he had not sought to take up. One such event stood out in his mind as emblematic of his frustration. This was a synod held in Rome in 1987; the topic was the role of the laity. After years of grassroots consultations, bishops from around the world had assembled in Rome with their position papers in hand, and the sentiment of their people on their minds, to discuss how much the laity, in a Church that had traditionally entrusted the dominant roles to clergy, should be allowed and expected to do. At the synod, Archbishop Weakland spoke plainly on the function of women in the Church. "Women who are loyal to and love the Church express dismay and discouragement if their talents and contributions to Church life are stifled or rejected," he said. "They want Church leaders to treat them as Jesus treated women. Women in the Gospels ministered to, with, and for Jesus." The Archbishop went on to advocate that women be allowed to assume all liturgical roles not requiring ordination, and that they be considered for openings in the Curia and the Vatican diplomatic corps.

"The consultation process beforehand took years," he told me. "Hundreds of thousands of people participated, in thousands of discussions, and many hundreds of documents were prepared, and the end result was so disappointing. After it was over, the Pope issued a statement, and, while it was not a bad statement, it really didn't go any further than what had already been said at Vatican II about the role of women in the Church. Who knows who subverts the process. The Pope? The Curia? But the Pope's document could have been written without the synod—without any of those extensive consultations. *Roma locuta est, causa finita est.* I vowed I would never go through such a charade again."

Rome has spoken, the case is closed; but this was Milwaukee, and this shepherd on the shores of Lake Michigan, far from the Tiber, had to continue to address the needs of his flock. One of his current concerns was a possible grim future of priestless parishes. Rome was clear on this point: the solution was prayer for more vocations; there would be no exceptions to a celibate male clergy; the shortage would pass. This did not satisfy Weakland, and for some time he had been mulling over the writing of a pastoral letter to the people of his archdiocese on the clerical crisis. Now he was beginning to see how it should be broken down. There would be three parts, the first two of which—with Scripture and Church tradition strategically employed—would lay out the problem. Part I would deal with the nature of the parish, Part II with the role of the priest. About Part III he was less certain, but he knew that what he had in mind to say could easily bring down the wrath of Rome. He needed time to think about it, and he set himself a deadline, so he would not indefinitely put off a difficult but necessary task. He decided to have a draft of the letter completed before he left Milwaukee, in early November, on the trip that would take him to Washington for the N.C.C.B. meeting, to Fribourg to accept the degree, and then on to El Salvador.

Archbishop Weakland has another, deeper medium by which to reach his people: the Mass. Catholicism is a liturgically based religion, and the Mass—in which Christ is sacramentally present in the Eucharist—is at its core. Masses are key events to gather the Milwaukee faithful, either those united by parish lines or those brought together by social or political concerns, and Archbishop Weakland uses such occasions for teaching, which he sees as a prelate's primary responsibility. Some within his archdiocese are open to his words; others regard him with profound distrust. Two such Masses, both held the same week in mid-October, particularly demonstrated for me the range of sentiment in the archdiocese.

One was a Children's Mass at Our Lady Queen of Peace, a church in a predominantly Polish section of Milwaukee's South Side. The church was built in 1988, in a starkly modern, modified Spanish-mission style. Its stained-glass windows, after a nod to the Old Testament (Moses), march triumphantly and with a certain ethnic bias through twenty centuries of Christianity (St. Peter; St. Adalbert, who is said to have brought Christianity to Poland, in the tenth century; Elizabeth Ann Seton, America's first native-born saint; and St. Maximilian Kolbe, who died in a Polish concentration camp) before boldly speculating on the twenty-first (John Paul II, who is both Polish and very much alive). Before Mass, the pastor and his associate chatted easily and amicably with the Archbishop as they vested in the sacristy. Even the altar boys seemed relaxed with him. One of them, a seventh grader named Jacob, was bemoaning the recent forced removal of a long lock of hair at the back of his head. "They call it a fag wag," he explained.

The Archbishop asked what that meant, and Jacob looked at him innocently and said, "I don't know. Just that I had to cut it off. Principal said so. We have rules. Can't have anything that calls attention to you."

"Hair," the Archbishop sighed. "See this skullcap? When I had enough hair, I had little combs inside to keep it on. One day, I put on the mitre — this big, stiff red hat I wear — a little crookedly and dug the combs right into my scalp. Ouch! Blood! Those days are over. Now the skullcap keeps slipping. Are you guys good basketball players? You might have to catch the mitre if it falls off."

When the Archbishop neared the altar and was about to greet his congregation — some three hundred school-children, the girls dressed in white blouses and plaid jumpers, the boys in dark trousers and pale-blue shirts — he was given a bouquet of yellow roses and a huge wall hanging of a rainbow drawn by the children and signed by all of them. After a short opening monologue on the symbolism of his ring, mitre, and shepherd's crook ("It's a cane, but with a hook on the end to rescue any of you little sheep that go astray"), he segued gracefully into the liturgy: "O.K. Let's begin Mass. Peace be with you. Now just relax, and ask God for all the graces you're going to need to be good today."

His homily began with a question: "How many of you have ever said, to your mom or dad, 'I love you — I think you're nice'?"

A full show of hands.

"Well, when you say it to God, what is that? Exactly. Prayer. That's what praying is, telling God He's nice. When you say 'Thank you, God' for something nice, that's praying, too. Now, let's see. You thank Him for — Hmmm. Ninja Turtles? Right! For homework? Nooo!"

The children, their broad Slavic faces smiling through much of the Mass, were a gratifyingly responsive group, obviously amazed and pleased that this towering personage, a majestic seven and a half feet tall in his red mitre, could be so plainspoken. At the Our Father, their pre-adolescent voices filled the church, and I found myself thinking that American Catholicism, with all its conflicts, vagaries, and shortcomings, with schools and parishes closing around the country, seemed strong and fruitful that morning at Queen of Peace.

The other Mass that week came complete with a title — "Respect Life: A Liturgical Celebration." It was held in the evening, in one of the archdiocese's wealthiest parishes, St. Jude the Apostle, in Wauwatosa. The Archbishop arrived at the rectory at five-thirty, in order to allow an hour between the planned dinner and the seven-thirty Mass — a fast required before the reception of Holy Eucharist. During dinner, the conversation with the pastor, Father Donald Weber, veered haltingly from one ecclesiastical subject to another, and painfully lacked the spontaneity of the Archbishop's visit to Queen of Peace. Father Weber spoke of his trip to Spain the preceding summer, and how impressed he had been by the shrine of the Virgin

Mary built there by Opus Dei, an ultraconservative lay and clerical religious society. The Archbishop smiled politely and offered a comment on the art of El Greco. Father Weber then noted with pride that his collection of relics continued to grow. In the room where the Archbishop later vested was a huge glass case containing two hundred and nineteen relics considered "first class"—bone fragments from a broad panoply of known and unknown Catholic saints. The Archbishop seemed not to notice the formidable presence of these holy particles. While he waited in the vestibule of the church for the procession to the altar, he was noticeably quiet, his gaze wandering over the magnificently plumed hats of the Knights of Columbus, who were to be his honor guard. Though he usually trades small talk with those in attendance at such functions, the Archbishop did not do so on this night; he returned the greetings and the proffered smiles but stood stiffly off to one side, an uncharacteristically frozen look on his face. When, finally, he reached the altar of the cavernous church, the Archbishop was almost lost to the eye before huge philodendrons and an ornate floor-to-ceiling mosaic framed in brass. Turning to face the congregation, he could see that the church was only half full. There were perhaps three hundred and fifty people in the pews. Two of them were reporters—Marie Rohde, from the Milwaukee *Journal*, and Mary Beth Murphy, from the *Sentinel*—who were there on assignment.

This was no ordinary evening Mass. It was the annual liturgical celebration held by the archdiocese's anti-abortion group. The sparse turnout could have been interpreted as a measure of the group's antipathy toward its archbishop, for this was normally a well-attended event.

Early the previous spring, as some bishops were threatening excommunication of politicians who supported a woman's right to an abortion and also of those working in abortion clinics—a threat actually carried out by Bishop Rene Gracida, of Corpus Christi, Texas, who excommunicated a clinic director and a clinic physician—Archbishop Weakland had taken another tack. He held six "listening sessions," in which Catholic women in Milwaukee were invited to air their views on the Church's stand on abortion. Catholic anti-abortion activists were enraged by this approach but temporarily held their fire. A few months later, in two long articles published in the archdiocesan newspaper, the Archbishop summed up and responded to what he had heard. Weakland wrote that while the women at the sessions saw abortion as a tragedy, they found the tactics of the pro-life movement "ugly and demeaning." Alluding to the common practice of handing out pictures of aborted fetuses, and the (less common) bombing of abortion clinics, the Archbishop wrote, "Many dislike the narrowness of so many in the pro-life movement, their tactics—their lack of compassion—their lack of civility," and he recommended that politicians unwilling to call for a ban on abortions be given "as much latitude as reason permits." As for the Church's ban on artificial means of birth control, a subject that had come up repeatedly during the listening sessions, he noted that "I did not sense that there was much support" for it.

The vast majority of Catholic priests and bishops are against abortion on demand, but few have lent their active support to the pro-life movement. Weakland was alone, however, in confronting its virulence head on. After his two articles appeared, the newspaper headlines—the *Sen-*

tinel's was "WEAKLAND: PRO-CHOICE COULD BE OK"—took some liberties with his actual stand, and the Archbishop was once more a national figure. While many applauded him, he quickly became the target of hate mail more rancorous and voluminous than any he had ever before received. The economic pastoral had brought hundreds of letters; these articles evoked thousands. He was called "butcher," "killer," "slaughterer," "murderer," and various unprintable names. The Catholic Center, which is a Washington-based group founded by Paul Weyrich, the tireless advocate of far-right causes, drew a parallel between Weakland and a German bishop who in 1933 became a member of the S.S. and "the apologist for Nazism among German Catholics," and it began a campaign to collect a hundred thousand signatures on a petition to the Apostolic pro-nuncio demanding that Weakland be disciplined.

That night at St. Jude's in Wauwatosa, Weakland's gestures during his homily were more expansive and nervous than usual, but his words were carefully chosen. "The dignity of every person is built in," he said. "Before birth, after birth, right to the last moment before death. The presumption is always in favor of life—so while civil authorities may say that capital punishment is allowable, we say that any taking of life is brutal, is wrong." Threads of the just-war theory, poverty, racism, social injustice were woven into a seamless cloth. He would not be drawn into addressing the single issue that his audience wanted him to discuss; instead, he offered an overarching argument for "a consistent life ethic." The word "abortion" never passed his lips. At the reception that followed, in the church hall, the Archbishop looked plainly exhausted by his attempts to walk such a fine line. He tried, and failed, to sustain small talk. On returning to his car, he found a flyer from a Philadelphia-based right-to-life group on the windshield in which, had he read it, he would have learned that he was a man who "abandons unborn children by rendering them invisible."

He sat quietly in the darkness of the back seat on the return trip to St. John's, and it was only when he mounted the stairs on the way to his rooms that he commented on the evening. "Such a difficult group to preach to," he said. "Such hard faces. Such surety. No smiles. No openness to any other point of view. But I really didn't handle it well. Too rhetorical. I wasn't well enough prepared, hadn't thought it out. They are a minority, they feel rejected. They have no joy in being Catholic or part of a Church. And there was a teaching moment. Missed." He flicked on the light. The smile came back, albeit wan and worn. "But you know what they really needed?" he asked. His look was at once mischievous and grandfatherly. "A laxative. And a hug."

O n another evening that October, I arrived at the Archbishop's rooms in the cathedral rectory to be greeted by Maria Callas's 1955 performance of "La Sonnambula," at La Scala, which was wafting into the study from his living room. "Her finest period," he said, and noted with blissful reverie and a touch of pride that he had heard her sing the work there. "That little 'action' I was thinking of might have to wait a bit," he continued, referring to the potentially troublesome third part of the pastoral letter addressing the shortage of priests. Professor Holderegger had phoned him from Fribourg to say that there had been an unforeseen hitch in the planned conferral of the honorary degree: the Vatican's Congregation for Catholic Education, which oversees ecclesiastically sanctioned schools of theology, like Fribourg's, had not yet approved Weakland's name. "And," the Archbishop added, in a tone as straightforward as it was unenthusiastic, "the new bishop of Green Bay has been named."

Although each bishop operates autonomously, dioceses in the United States are grouped into thirty-three provinces. The Wisconsin province, of which Milwaukee's archbishop is the titular head, includes the state's four other dioceses — Green Bay, La Crosse, Madison, and Superior.

In this arrangement, the archbishop holds the title of metropolitan, and periodically brings together the four other diocesan bishops—called suffragans—and the four auxiliary bishops (one each in Madison and Green Bay and two in Milwaukee). While a metropolitan's recommendations for the appointment of bishops within his province, and for new bishops to be raised up from the ranks of his priests, are no more than that—the Pope reserves the right to name whomever he likes—his word is commonly held to carry a weight commensurate with his standing in Rome. New York's Cardinal John O'Connor is considered the prime bishop-maker in America, followed by Boston's Cardinal Bernard Law; Washington's Cardinal James Hickey; Cardinal John Krol, the former head of the Philadelphia archdiocese; and the two latest appointees to the College of Cardinals—Roger Mahony, of Los Angeles, and Anthony Bevilacqua, of Philadelphia. By contrast, Archbishop Weakland's suggestions for new leadership in his province have been ignored; moreover, it has been eleven years since a priest of the archdiocese of Milwaukee has been consecrated a bishop.

The process of naming bishops within the Catholic Church is a fascinating mixture of transcendent vision and politics of varying degrees of venality. Sometimes the best men are named—the brightest, or the most pastoral, or those who are beloved by fellow-clerics and by the people and are thus able to lead them most effectively. More often the choice falls on men whose views mesh with those of the current Pope, and whose allegiance can therefore be depended on. At its most venal, the process provides a reward—for, say, an American ethnic group that has raised a huge sum of money for the Vatican and expects to see the purple zucchetto on the head of one of its own, or for an Italian family with centuries of ties to the papacy. In the past, concordats or other agreements with several countries have stipulated that the Vatican would allow them a voice in choosing their bishops. America's first bishop, John Carroll, was elected by his fellow-priests, in 1789, and up until the First Vatican Council, in 1869-70 — a gathering that declared the doctrine of papal infallibility, thus consolidating Rome's power—local churches, and even civil authorities, had significant input. But the days of such modest participation are over. The current Pope appoints his own choices, acknowledging but often disregarding local sentiment, and unfettered by checks and balances. So much power in the naming of members of the Catholic hierarchy has never been wielded before.

The new man for the diocese of Green Bay was Bishop Robert Banks, a sixty-two-year-old auxiliary in Boston, who had worked closely with Cardinal Law. When his appointment was made official, the Milwaukee *Journal* called it "a papal slap in the face" for Weakland. The Archbishop brushed this off as "journalism," but if it was not a slap in the face it was surely one on the wrist. Banks had the reputation of being conservative in matters of dogma—he and Law had recently led an anti-abortion march in Boston—and his appointment was viewed both in the local papers and in the national Catholic press as an antidote to the progressivism that Weakland had come to espouse. Weakland's statement to the press skirted the issue, extolling the people, not the appointee: "He will find the Church here a vibrant one. In particular, he will see that his own diocese of Green Bay is full of devout Catholics, eager for enlightened leadership." Privately, the

Archbishop's views were considerably less complacent. He feared that the appointment would cause a severe morale problem among the Green Bay priests, who had been serving under one of their own—Auxiliary Bishop Robert Morneau—since June, when Green Bay's former bishop, Adam Maida, was named the archbishop of Detroit. Morneau had been the unanimous choice of Weakland and the other Wisconsin-province bishops, and it was Morneau's name they had sent to the Vatican by way of the nuncio, who may well have tabled it.

The "unforeseen hitch" complicating the Fribourg honorary degree looked like another Vatican slap, yet Weakland showed no disappointment or anger over either development. The Vatican was holding up what is usually pro-forma approval, and someone viewed as a consecrated carpetbagger—something of a Vatican mole—was being planted in his province; nevertheless, the Archbishop went on with his work, with no more than an occasional mention of either apparent slight. Four priests had recently sent letters of resignation to the chancery; alcohol, a woman, bitterness with the Church, and mental illness had respectively overcome their callings. A parish with no future was asking for twenty thousand dollars to keep it functioning. The archdiocesan director of the Respect Life Office had resigned, saying that she could no longer "perpetuate the myth" that the archdiocese was committed to anti-abortion efforts. Pastoral associates—in many cases nuns, who are called upon to perform non-sacramental functions such as sick calls, catechetical instruction, and pre-marriage counselling—were being appointed by pastors to help ease the burden on parish priests; yet there was no established procedure to oversee their qualifications or to exercise control over where they were appointed. House-keepers have been known to follow a pastor through a succession of parish assignments like surrogate wives, and Weakland did not want this new class of associates to begin such a pattern.

As for matters of more personal concern, the Little Eucharistic Lamb had called the Archbishop one evening at the cathedral rectory, having somehow obtained his private number. She said that she was in a phone booth across the street and had seen his car return to the garage; she had then waited to see the lights go on in his rooms. She pressed the Archbishop to perform an exorcism, saying that she was in continuous, excruciating pain. She had just seen the movie "Dick Tracy," she said, in which she had detected a plot to assassinate the Pope. She went on to link a character in it named Eighty-eight Keys with a bishop of "the dissident church." This bishop, she said, was a dangerous man, and might be involved in the assassination plot. It was probably just a coincidence, but Weakland had been nicknamed Eighty-eight Keys during his seminary days, because of his proficiency at the piano. The Lamb had also begun to attend the Archbishop's Sunday-morning Mass. On the advice of the psychologist leading the evaluation team that was trying to schedule an interview with the woman, the Archbishop had hired two plain-clothes female guards from a private security agency, and directed them to sit in the pew behind her to prevent any disruptive action on her part.

Perhaps most disturbing was a phone call from Eileen Purcell, the executive director of the SHARE Foundation, which was coordinating the forthcoming El Salvador trip. She informed the Archbishop that one of the rural communities they were to visit had been the scene of an ambush a few days earlier. Father Jon de Cortina, a colleague of the six Jesuits killed by Salvadoran Army soldiers the previous November, had been held down for an hour and a half by sniper fire. One bullet had passed through the roof of his car, and another had hit the doorframe inches from his face, before he was able to get out and run for cover. Some forty-five shots in all had been fired. The Archbishop asked whether it was just a scare tactic or whether the snipers had meant to kill Father Cortina. It was not just a scare tactic, Purcell replied. But the trip was still on.

On a Tuesday, the Archbishop's day off, we took a stroll by Lake Michigan, which is a leisurely ten-minute walk from the rectory. It was an unseasonably warm day, and Weakland was dressed in a beige cardigan, a green-plaid sports shirt, and tan slacks — an outfit that made him look more like a banker or an insurance agent in early retirement than like an archbishop.

"Let's talk about this Church of ours," he said, sitting down on one of the benches overlooking the lake. "But first let's back up a bit — two Popes and two nuncios ago — to trace why Weakland is held in such high regard by our friends in Rome. I was appointed in 1977 by Pope Paul VI, in the aftermath of Vatican II — its reverberations were still being felt, though it had ended twelve years before. Pope John XXIII had been warned that chaos follows councils — and that was indeed true for the council he called and, sadly, did not live long enough to see completed. But the feeling within at least some parts of the Vatican — and certainly with Paul VI, who succeeded John XXIII — was that the changes were for the best. A Church more responsive to modern needs was emerging. At the time, the Apostolic delegate in America was Archbishop Jean Jadot, and Jadot was looking for priests and auxiliaries who would be the most effective—and this is important—*pastors*. Not administrators or theologians or canonists but pastors. Bishops throughout America knew that Jadot would listen to them and would forward their requests to Rome. So we saw a wonderful flowering of open, pastoral, and, by the way, popular men: Howard Hubbard to Albany, Matt Clark to Rochester, William Borders to Baltimore, Anthony Pilla to Cleveland, Walter Sullivan to Richmond.

"Paul VI died the year after I was appointed. John Paul I lived for only a month or so after his election, and then our current Pope, John Paul II, was elected. It was a brilliant choice—this man from an Iron Curtain country—and I was very enthusiastic about what he would do. John Paul II knew what it was like to live under oppression, and so he brought to office a certain toughness and a desire for discipline—things that keep people together when they are forced to tolerate an oppressive political system. He felt that the Church had gone too far, and, basically, he was right. It was time to slow things down, absorb the changes, see what was working and what was not. He is a strong man, with definite ideas, and he felt that he needed to take control of a rudderless ship.

"He looked to America and found that all these popular, pastoral bishops, appointed before his time, were going off in various directions and were not in step with Rome. The American conference of bishops had begun to practice the principles that we are used to in a democratic society. But the Church is not a democratic institution, and the Pope wanted to restore control to the Vatican. The Popes who had appointed these pastoral bishops were dead. Jadot, the man who had recommended many of them, was still the nuncio, but his judgment was no longer trusted. He was soon replaced by Archbishop Pio Laghi, whose judgment the Pope could trust. Laghi's mandate was to find men for the hierarchy who would put the Church back on track—men who would listen to and be obedient to Rome. As for Jadot, his reward was a low-level job in the Vatican. Although every American nuncio before him had eventually been made a cardinal, he was not.

"When it became apparent to me what the years under John Paul II would be like, I didn't sit down and line up any master plan of confrontation for the next few decades. That was Rome; I was Milwaukee. I had my own work to do, and, just as I had done as abbot and then as primate, I simply went about my business, listening to what people were saying, watching the tide of human events. But if you are the least bit sensitive to what is happening around you, and a situation presents itself that is not right, you have to do your best to say or do something about it. Regardless of whom it pleases or displeases. Take the appointment of Dick Sklba. The Wisconsin province had recommended Father Richard Sklba as an auxiliary bishop for the Milwaukee archdiocese, and in 1979 the word came down that he was about to be named. The priests of Milwaukee were ecstatic. Everybody loved Sklba, both as a priest and as the rector of our seminary. Then, between the time of the announcement and the date of his consecration, I got a phone call: the Vatican was going to cancel the appointment. Not long before, Sklba had chaired a Catholic Biblical Association committee that was charged with examining whether Holy Scripture precluded the ordination of women. In his rather lengthy report was a line or two stating that Scripture in fact did not preclude women priests, and pointing out that the fact that the Apostles were all men couldn't in itself be used to defend an all-male clergy. He in no way advocated the ordination of women; he merely rendered his scholarly judgment on various recurrent arguments. And because of this the Vatican was going to undo him.

"I couldn't let this happen. Should a line or two in a document that really didn't go very far be allowed to ruin a man's life? I called Rome and told them that Dick and I were coming over and wanted to see the Pope. When we got there, Cardinal Casaroli, his secretary of state, said that I was too angry and the Pope was too angry for a meeting to do any good. Instead, he asked us to draft some sort of statement, acceptable to the Pope, that would in essence have Sklba back down from his position. We drafted something—not a backing down but an attempt to put Sklba's statement in the context of Church teaching— and the word came back that the Pope said no. We drafted another statement and waited. Dick was to be consecrated on a Wednesday in Milwaukee; it was now Saturday in Rome, and we had a Sunday-morning flight home. Finally, late Saturday night, we got word that the Pope had approved, but with the stipulation that the statement appear in the Milwaukee papers on Tuesday, the day before Sklba's consecration. Well, the papers not only didn't play the statement as Sklba backing down but gave it the angle that he stood behind what he had originally written. We sent the articles on to Rome, but, fortunately, it being the pre-fax era, they didn't arrive in time for Rome to respond. So, while Sklba's career was certainly stalemated right off the bat, he was consecrated a bishop.

"That incident, obviously, made Rome distrustful of me. And I imagine that other stands I have taken—from advocating a fuller role for women in the Church to what I have said about abortion—do not correspond with what the Vatican wants put forward. On the abortion issue: Can you, as a Catholic, be personally against abortion, yet, as an elected representative or private citizen, allow abortions to be done? That is a very big question for me, and, frankly, one for which I still don't have an answer. But I do know that you cannot take away a person's right to make a wrong decision. There may be a Church ideal—an ideal that we would like everyone to live up to—but my job is to funnel down what comes from the Vatican and find out what Joe Blow in front of me needs in order to survive, what can reasonably be asked of him. This is what being pastoral is about."

Over the years Archbishop Weakland has continually spoken out against the professed preeminence of his church. "The church as a 'perfect society' is a fake," he said in a speech. "The church is a broken society . . . we minister as broken people." He lashed out at a "new Augustinianism" in the church—an allusion to St. Augustine's "City of God," a flawless, church-centered society which stood in apposition to a degraded, secular world occupied with its own concerns—that would "get rid of the divorced and gays in order to live in a perfect world." The media branded him a liberal, an appellation he denies, calling himself "very much a centrist." In one of his *Catholic Herald* columns he wrote, "The extreme right offers more security and the extreme left more excitement, but common sense usually dictates a certain balance and a middle course that provides, in the end, steady and sure progress."

A jogger thumped past as we sat by the lake, and he and the Archbishop exchanged waves. It was a brilliantly clear and windy day. Inside the breakwater, huge cargo ships stood at anchor, awaiting berthing space in the Port of Milwaukee, while the few sailboat captains brave enough to face the choppy waters found themselves heeled over to the gunwales. Toward the west, the not very imposing Milwaukee skyline broke the horizon.

"Again let me say I agree with the Pope—things have gone too far," the Archbishop continued after a moment. "But his position of either-or, clamping down on dissent wherever he senses it, doesn't really clarify or help. I believe in a both-and Church. There is a natural tension built into Christianity. The Church has always struggled to preserve the purity of the Gospel in the light of a changing world. It is the age-old struggle to combine human truth—wherever it is found—with the revealed truth that comes from God. But I think history shows that we need not fear new thoughts or new discoveries. In the early days of the Church, when the Gospel, which was born into an earthy, Jewish culture, had to face the Hellenistic, or neo-Platonic, dualistic thinking, it finally evolved a deeper vision of this world, where salvation is worked out in relation to the next. In the fifth century, this thinking culminated in Augustine, who—afraid to accept what seemed to him the merely human in art and knowledge—created the thesis of two separate 'cities.' It seemed like a perfect vision, and it lasted for centuries in the West. But, in the thirteenth century, theologians like St. Thomas Aquinas—who, by the way, was considered a heretic in his time—had to face the new influences of Aristotelian thinking that had reached the West through the Arabic philosophers, like Averroes and Avicenna. Out of that challenge came the idea that the supernatural is really built on the natural, and doesn't deny it. *Nihil humanum mihi alienum est.* 'Nothing human is foreign to me.' The Renaissance brought a new humanism, putting the accent on the human body. The Church, aghast at first, absorbed this new art, in its Raphael, its Michelangelo, even its Titian and Tintoretto. The Enlightenment of the eighteenth century, with its accent on human reason, posed special problems for the Church. The Enlightenment terrified the Church with the revolutionary idea that there could be double truths—opposed, but each true. Rousseau, Locke, Hobbes posited that problems could be solved by human reason, and reason became a god in itself. Science blossomed. And God's mysterious ways were explained away by reason and by science. Galileo's contention that the earth revolved around the sun, which contradicted the first chapter of Genesis—was that worthy of excommunication? Now we can see that the two are not contradictory. Darwin and the origin of species, Freud and the workings of the psyche? If there is truth, it will win out and be integrated into the revealed. If an idea is false, it will fall away. It makes no sense to do battle with new ideas just because they don't seem to fit neat little categories that might have been codified by some council hundreds of years ago.

"But the glory of the Church is that it does eventually accept and grow. Ideas from the Enlightenment gradually entered into the Church's thinking. For example, when Pope Leo XIII published *Rerum Novarum*, in 1891, he relied as much on the theories of individual rights of a Locke as he did on the common-good concepts of an Aquinas. The Second Vatican Council, in documents like *Dignitatis Humanae*—written in consultation with the American theologian John Courtney Murray—came to terms with the Enlightenment and proclaimed the importance of the individual conscience in religion. *Dignitatis Humanae* stated that one's conscience is inviolable and that no one should be forced to worship against his conscience. It is an incredible document. But, ah—." The Archbishop paused.

I was glad of the respite: Weakland's journey through Church, philosophical, and scientific history had flowed without hesitation for the past twenty minutes, and I had been struggling to take it all in.

"The issues today?" he went on. "Sexuality—that's the big one. We haven't come to terms with it at all. Our scientific understanding is still rudimentary. Normal sexual drives, homosexuality, pedophilia. Contraception—the fact that science can control or modify human reproduction. It is a great and frightening frontier, the Galileo issue of our day. And the Church is reluctant to accept the results of the human sciences; instead, it harks back to the days when you could say, 'This is black, this is white; this right, this wrong.' Another challenge we face is the dialectic between what we as Catholics believe and what we practice, and the decision about what of our moral code should be incorporated into the legal code. This is especially relevant in America, because we are the first generation of Catholics to be in the mainstream here. What are we asking our society to do?

"For me personally, the most interesting and difficult area has to do with relationships—that very tired word. The early asceticism of the Church—asceticism that I was brought up in and practiced—was about domesticating yourself, getting control of yourself. We were soldiers fighting under a banner, and mutual support was the key to reaching a higher good. For a person like me — a control person, who likes things measured, predictable — it was great. But the world has changed. This age is asking us to relate to each other and not only to that safe banner — to make sacrifices not only for the cause but for each other. In essence, we are being asked to let things get out of control. This is the new asceticism: living with imperfection. And, believe me, it is harder than wearing hair shirts and spending hours on your knees in prayer. Especially for me, God knows.

"But I have made the decision that I cannot control the world around me, and I'm trying very hard to live with that in myself and in my Church. And perhaps it's what gives me a certain detachment about what is going on. Because, after all, these are exciting days — somewhat like the golden age of the fifth-century Church, when people were excited about religion, and it was constantly debated in the public forum. I believe you can remain faithful to the Church while continually challenging it. If the Fribourg degree is denied — that's such a pitifully small matter. Who will be the poorer for it, me or the Curia? Yes, I'm sure they are thinking up ways to keep me in line, to criticize me, isolate me. I would do the same thing to someone who was causing me problems. Nobody likes someone standing up to him and challenging what he says. I surely don't. So my career is over. I will die the Archbishop of Milwaukee. Nothing wrong with that at all. But to get worked up over something like Fribourg, to feel bad about it? To look over my shoulder and wonder if Rome will be pleased with what I say?" He shrugged, cocked his head to the side, and, bending his arms at the elbow, held up his palms to Heaven. I was reminded of the statue of Pope Paul VI that looks on benignly in the Archbishop's office.

T hree weeks before Archbishop Weakland was to go to the N.C.C.B. meeting in Washington, he had a phone call from Rome. Father Damian Byrne, the master general of the Dominican order, which administers Fribourg's theological school, called to say that the Vatican had finally spoken, and that the answer was no. Fribourg had been denied permission to grant him a degree. Two Swiss bishops, a Swiss Benedictine abbot, and the secretary of the Swiss bishops' conference had flown to the Vatican to intercede with Archbishop Pio Laghi, whose congregation was withholding permission. Laghi told them flatly that "it would not be wise" to honor Weakland. When pressed, Laghi said that he had received "protests from a strong pro-life group in New York" concerning the Weakland degree.

The Archbishop of Milwaukee pondered what action to take, if any. He met with his two auxiliary bishops, Richard Sklba and Leo Brust. They advised him not to acquiesce but, rather, to try to clear his name with Rome. Father Roland Trauffer, the secretary of the Swiss bishops' conference, said that while he was putting no pressure on Weakland to withdraw, such a move would make life considerably easier for the Swiss Church, which was having problems with the Vatican similar to Weakland's: Rome had just appointed to the diocese of Chur a bishop who was not being accepted by the people and the priests. After this conversation, Weakland made a decision. Although his withdrawal would, as he said it, "put the shadow on my shoulders, not the Vatican's," he would remove his name from consideration.

Events moved quickly after that. The Theology Faculty of Fribourg decided that it would grant no honorary degrees at all, and drastically scaled down what was to have been a grand centennial commemoration. These actions left the Archbishop in a rather peculiar position. He knew that the American press would get wind of this latest censure of him by Rome, and he considered calling a few of his press contacts—Peter Steinfels, the senior religion correspondent for the New York *Times*; Tom Fox, the editor of the *National Catholic Reporter*; and the religion writers for the *Journal* and the *Sentinel*—but decided against it. He did not want to be the one to point the finger at Rome. Although he had no intention of publicly divulging the information that he was receiving, on an almost daily basis, from friends in the Vatican and from the Swiss involved in the Fribourg affair (much of it was hearsay, and Vatican gossip is at once among the juiciest and the least reliable in the world), Weakland had some potentially inflammatory material. "A strong pro-life group in New York" was thought by his sources to mean— or, at least, to include—Cardinal John O'Connor. As an American whom Rome trusts, the Cardinal was a logical source of advice concerning Weakland. It was not thought that O'Connor had in any way campaigned against the degree; merely an unenthusiastic mention of Weakland's "listening sessions" on abortion could have signalled his sentiments. The hand of Cardinal Joseph Ratzinger was also suspected by a number of Weakland's contacts, since Weakland had voluntarily sent his two controversial articles in the *Catholic Herald* on the listening sessions to Ratzinger and his Congregation for the Doctrine of the Faith.

The Archbishop kept his counsel, but in early November the story leaked out. Ethel Gintoft, the executive editor of the *Catholic Herald*, had found out about Fribourg through the chancery grapevine, and she confronted Weakland with her knowledge. Unlike many American bishops, who use their diocesan newspapers as official mouthpieces, Weakland had given her free rein to cover and write about whatever she considered news to the people of the archdiocese. The Archbishop knew that the word would now spread quickly, so he called Steinfels, Fox, and the local reporters, and then flew to Washington. He was uneasy about the fact that the story would break as the nation's bishops were convening, but relieved that he could go directly on to El Salvador.

Part II

❧{ **WASHINGTON** }❧

rchbishop Weakland was on his way from Milwaukee to Washington to attend the annual meeting of the National Conference of Catholic Bishops, itself one of many innovations that arose from the Second Vatican Council, which convened in 1962 and concluded in 1965. The intent of the Council was to move the Catholic Church away from a strict hierarchical authoritarianism, so that a "people of God" might inform the Church with its collective wisdom and spirit. Laypeople, once regarded as little more than vulnerable souls to be protected and saved, were now looked upon as the building blocks of new communities of faith, and the bishops of the Church—who had operated largely independently of one another within their various sees, in direct fealty to the Pope—were asked to band together in national conferences. In pre-Council days, there had been little need for bishops to consult with one another, because of the Church's rigorous uniformity: the same Mass, said in Latin around the globe, was emblematic of religious unity, and a point of pride, while a standardized doctrine demanded obedience and brooked no dissenting interpretation. The new national bishops' conferences were to be the means of carrying out Vatican II reforms, and were also meant to provide a forum for bishops to present what the people in the pews were saying about current Church practice. With input from above and below, bishops could then best discern what God wanted of His Church at that moment in its history. Accordingly, in 1966 the American bishops voted to form two groups: the National Conference of Catholic Bishops, which would attend to Church matters, and a parallel group, the United States Catholic Conference, to address secular issues.

After Vatican II, the Catholic Church basked for a time in the ecclesiastical equivalent of a Prague Spring. Mass was offered in the vernacular, and altars were uprooted and turned around, so that the priest faced the congregants. The private reading of the Bible by the untutored faithful, which had once been discouraged as a suspect activity, was now advocated. It became easier for priests and other religious to receive dispensation from their vows (if, indeed, they chose to take the formal route), and annulments of marriages became less remarkable and easier to obtain. Parish councils assumed many of the tasks that once only a pastor could perform.

Though the reforms persist, the atmosphere the Council engendered has changed dramatically, as a result of three events closely spaced in the long history of the Church: the publication, in 1968, of the papal encyclical *Humanae Vitae*; the election, in 1978, of Pope John Paul II; and the installation, in 1981, of a key member of the Curia. *Humanae Vitae*, disregarding the advice of many medical experts and a number of Church theologians, reaffirmed the Church's ban on all forms of artificial birth control. Instead of receiving a resounding chorus of Amens and Alleluias from bishops around the world, the Vatican quickly discovered that its newly enfranchised middle managers could no longer be relied upon to toe the line, especially when confronted with an unpopular document built on a disputable theological foundation. The national bishops' conferences affirmed *Humanae Vitae*, but the affirmations ranged from a firm "yes" to acknowledgments so nuanced by exceptions as to virtually neutralize the document. Several of the national conferences — in particular, those of the United States, Canada, France, and the Netherlands — held that the thoughtful, prayerful Catholic could disregard this teaching and still remain in communion with Rome.

And there was a change in the character of the Vatican itself, with the election of John Paul II, and his appointment of the conservative German cardinal Joseph Ratzinger as prefect of the Congregation for the Doctrine of the Faith. The new Pope's experience with national bishops' conferences had been predominantly with those of Eastern Europe, whose bishops prided themselves on their concerted opposition to oppressive Communist regimes while, ironically, accepting without question the edicts of Rome. The Polish Pope soon found that he had inherited many fractious and outspoken groups, America's among them. He could hardly disinherit or disband the bishops' conferences, but his task, as he saw it, was clear: to reassert the Pope's primacy as the sole source of authoritative teaching, and to once again standardize Catholic practice, which John Paul regarded as dangerously out of control.

The N.C.C.B. was perhaps the most vexing group. Bishops' conferences throughout the world are conducted with varying degrees of openness; a few are held entirely in private. But the N.C.C.B.'s meetings are open to the press — a press whose words and images are seen worldwide – and the Vatican realized that their influence was immediate and formidable. Rome could not openly control the N.C.C.B. agenda, but it could blunt the group's impact by casting all the bishops' conferences as merely consultative bodies and vesting more power in the Curia – a smaller body, whose members could be more easily watched over and swayed. Nearly three decades after Vatican II, the ecclesiastical power of national bishops' conferences remains unclear. Many prelates – Rembert Weakland among them – consider the conferences an authentic teaching voice, an extension of the historic episcopal authority to teach the truths of religion. Cardinal Ratzinger, however, has baldly maintained that they have little, if any, ecclesiastical base and therefore no ecclesiastical power. In Ratzinger's view – which is shared, not incidentally, by his Pope – the role of the bishops' conferences is simply to fine-tune and promulgate policy, not to make it.

While the N.C.C.B. has at times been one of the most progressive of the bishops' conferences, it has always been characterized by conflicting interests. From the outset, there were those bishops who feared that the N.C.C.B. would weaken what had once been complete and unquestioned dominion in their home dioceses and impose a barrier between themselves and the authority conferred on them by Rome. These men felt that their allegiance to the Pope was primary and sacred, and they fought the conference concept, looking to Rome rather than to their fellow-bishops or to the people of their dioceses for counsel and guidance. When a controversial issue was under debate in the N.C.C.B.'s early days, the late Cardinal John Cody, of Chicago, for one, could rise to his feet and proclaim, "I was on the telephone just yesterday with the Curia about this, and they said—." "For men like Cody, whose vision of the Church was one of centralized divine power—and for a number of like-minded clergy who, moreover, aspired to Vatican positions—the hand of Rome was to be reached for and tightly clasped. Cody's open autocratism and bullying would be anathema in today's seemingly more consensus-conscious Church, but Rome's influence is felt in subtler ways, more and more frequently, as the Vatican seeks to regain control over what it considers a Church in extremis.

Never in the American Church's history have the beliefs and practices of the people been more at odds with the teachings that Rome espouses and local bishops are supposed to promote, the question of birth control being only the best known of many examples. Survey after survey has revealed that the majority of this country's Catholics, who number fifty-eight million, profess allegiance to the Pope yet refuse to live by his decrees, and the American bishops converging on the Omni Shoreham Hotel in Washington on the second Sunday of November for the N.C.C.B.'s four-day meeting were well aware of the disaffection in the ranks.

Archbishop Weakland spent much of that Sunday in his room at the Shoreham, slogging through six hundred and sixty-two pages of documents containing the twenty "action items" — those to be voted on — and thirty-two "information items" on the meeting's agenda. To the casual observer, the range might have appeared quite broad: a statement on human sexuality, a proposal to allow laypeople to officiate at funerals, a report on ways to introduce "inclusive" (i.e., non-sexist) language into the liturgy, a proclamation to place feast days honoring the Blessed Miguel Agustín Pro and the Blessed Juan Diego (two men on their way to sainthood and especially venerated by Mexican-Americans) on the American Church calendar. But to Weakland it was largely a study in clerical housekeeping, and tardy housekeeping at that. Years before, the Milwaukee archdiocese had adopted inclusive language. In the sensitive area of gay rights, Milwaukee had, in essence, ducked a major controversy. In 1988, after the Vatican moved to ban the Catholic homosexual group Dignity from holding public Masses, a suburban Milwaukee church that had been holding such Masses instituted one that gays consider their own, although it is not held under the Dignity banner.

One of the most controversial issues facing the American Church was not even on the agenda. A proposed pastoral letter on the status of women in the Church, which had been in the works for seven years, had been so roundly criticized for its tepidness by both liberals and conservatives (Weakland had recommended scuttling it outright) that it had been sent back to committee. Weakland had commissioned a study in 1982 on the status of women in his archdiocese, and he had subsequently integrated women into virtually all levels of church work there. Not a man to fight public battles he has already privately won, the Archbishop knew that he would have little to say at the meeting.

That morning's New York *Times* had carried a story by Peter Steinfels about the Vatican's refusal to approve an honorary degree for Weakland from the Theology Faculty of the University of Fribourg, which wanted to recognize the Archbishop for his central role in the drafting of a pastoral letter on the American economy that the N.C.C.B. had issued in 1986. Steinfels noted that the Vatican, in barring the university from awarding the degree, had asserted that Weakland's "statements on abortion had caused 'a great deal of confusion among the faithful,' " and the article continued:

Last spring Archbishop Weakland held hearings with women in the Milwaukee archdiocese to gather their views on abortion. In a widely publicized report after the sessions, he upheld the Catholic teaching that abortion is immoral but warned that the anti-abortion movement was driving away potential supporters, including Catholics, who viewed its focus as narrow, its tactics as aggressive and some of its rhetoric as "ugly and demeaning." [Weakland] added that his hearings had revealed "how far the gap is between the official teaching" of the church prohibiting the use of birth control and the views of "some very conscientious women."

He also stated that moral principles could not be a matter of law unless they enjoyed "a consensus of the population."

Steinfels further noted, "Symbolic rebukes like this one are often used by the Vatican to show who is in the good graces of papal officials and who is not. Bishops are considered to be the successors of the first apostles, and direct papal measures against them are unusual."

On forays through the Shoreham's lobby that day to take a break from his reading, Weakland was approached by a good many of his fellow-bishops who had seen the story. All were supportive, as was to be expected; more remarkable was the undercurrent of astonishment at the Vatican's clumsy handling of the matter. During one such excursion, Weakland saw New York's Cardinal John O'Connor across the Shoreham lobby. Although he knows O'Connor reasonably well, he made an effort to avoid eye contact, more because of embarrassment that O'Connor might be feeling than from any discomfort of his own. Weakland had heard from a colleague that the New York *Post* had called O'Connor — a militant opponent of abortion — the day before to say that unnamed Vatican sources had suggested that input from him had helped to jinx Weakland's Fribourg degree. Upon spotting Weakland, the Cardinal rushed across the lobby to him and took him aside. "I want you to know that I had absolutely nothing to do with this, Rembert," he said gravely, keeping hold of Weakland's arm as he spoke. "It's libellous, downright libellous, I tell you!"

Weakland gave O'Connor's hand a pat and smiled. "Don't be worried about it, John—I'm not," he replied. Moments later, to another prelate, Weakland observed with a laugh that he had made the *Times* twice in one year for doing nothing: first for listening to other people discuss abortion and now for not receiving an honorary degree.

That evening, as he and I sat together in the Shoreham's lobby, the full impact of the Vatican's refusal seemed to have sunk in. He was hardly morose, and he didn't seem resentful; he evinced, instead, a certain bewilderment. "I feel a little bit like I've been raped," he said. "I feel dirty, and I don't know why."

Did he believe O'Connor's protestations?

"I have no reason to doubt him, but"—he gazed somewhat bemusedly across the lobby, which was filled with more men in black suits than the hotel would ordinarily see in a full year—"I didn't hear him say anything about my getting a raw deal. Or anything about standing with me on this."

A lthough there were briefings and committee meetings throughout Sunday, the conference officially began with a concelebrated Mass in the hotel's Palladian Room on Monday morning at eight o'clock. Some three hundred of the nation's bishops were present, and they were an impressive legion as they stood shoulder to shoulder before their gray metal folding chairs, row upon row of purple zucchettos, with a sprinkling of scarlet zucchettos (denoting the rank of cardinal), on heads bowed in prayer. Their deliberations would take place in three-hour sessions over the next three mornings and afternoons—sessions allotting minimum time for the consideration of each issue, in order to cover the maximum number of issues.

The sessions took place in the hotel's cavernous Regency Ballroom, which was brilliantly lit to allow complete live coverage by the Eternal Word Television Network. The bishops were seated at long tables set up at angles, like so many ribs of a fish (an arrangement that called to mind the ancient symbol of Christ), all of them in regulation black suits, some with their pectoral crosses tucked into shirt pockets, so that only a few links of gold chain hinted at the power that those symbols of office represent. The picture of catholicity was somewhat skewed, however: there were only a few black and a few Hispanic faces among them, and no Asian faces at all. Basically, the N.C.C.B. reflects the composition of the American Church a few decades ago—largely Irish, German, Italian, and Eastern European. Nonetheless, when the meeting began any monolithic quality that might have been projected to the world outside was soon dispelled. These were individuals, each with his own understanding of his job, his own "management style," his own attitude toward the power structure in Rome, his own political beliefs and leanings, his own concept of the pathways to holiness.

In the first working session, on Monday morning, the temporal and immediate intruded on the eternal and spiritual in the form of the Persian Gulf crisis. At that time, American troops were poised in Saudi Arabia but had not yet engaged the Iraqis in Kuwait. Archbishop Roger Mahony, of Los Angeles, asked for fifteen minutes at the podium. As the head of the United States Catholic Conference's International Policy Committee, he had already sent Secretary of State James Baker a letter in which he voiced his concern that "the pressure to use military force may grow as the pursuit of nonviolent options almost inevitably becomes difficult, complex, and slow," and he urged the bishops to accept the letter as their statement against war in the Gulf. For some, like Bishop Michael Kenny, of Juneau, Mahony's bold action—which had earned him the displeasure of his fellow-conservatives, who could usually count upon Mahony and now felt betrayed—was not bold enough, and a much stronger letter was needed. Kenny, boyish-looking in the midst of so many gray-haired and balding men, told the tall, patrician Mahony that if their

Church had no compunctions about condemning abortion it should offer equally unambiguous guidance on this serious moral question. For others, like Boston's Cardinal Bernard Law, to send any sort of letter opposing war was to ask too much of the nation's leaders at a time of crisis. Law, a huge, white-haired man whose gentle voice would often be heard throughout the conference, coming over the public-address system almost as an intimate whisper and often granting the liberal point of view before propounding his own, suggested that further debate be confined to the bishops' single executive session—a closed meeting, to be held Wednesday afternoon—and that the conference move on. Law's motion seemed to fail in the voice vote that followed, but, curiously, when written ballots were called for, it passed. With this halting exchange, the meeting got under way, having relegated to private reflection a matter that was then at the center of noisy public debate.

With action on the Persian Gulf postponed, the bishops turned back to the affairs of their state. The first significant debate came on Tuesday morning, on a measure that would permit laypeople to preside at funerals when a priest was not available. Such a practice is provisionally allowed by canon law; a regional conference of bishops need only ask Rome for the exception. Many voices were raised in a now familiar complaint: priests are overburdened to the point of exhaustion and ineffectuality by the plethora of rituals that only they are entitled to perform. Nevertheless, Pittsburgh's Bishop Donald Wuerl came to the podium to tell his colleagues to stand firm—that new vocations would come. Wuerl, whom the Vatican once sent to Seattle to temper Archbishop Raymond Hunthausen's

efforts to liberalize Church practice, is a telegenic figure —
a rising young hierarchical star who has his own television
show, on which he occasionally wears a short purple cloak
called a mozzetta over his bishop's cassock, with its red
piping and brilliant red sash, evoking for some viewers
memories of the glory days of Bishop Fulton J. Sheen. He
spoke of how "precious" the priesthood was, and how the
proposed measure would "send out the wrong signal" both
to the faithful and to prospective seminarians. Robert
Banks, the new Bishop of Green Bay—whom the Pope
had appointed in disregard of the candidate Weakland
had recommended—took the floor to reinforce Wuerl's
argument. Weakland himself, in the first of three short
appearances at the microphone, took the opposing view,
speaking in favor of allowing members of the laity to officiate and noting that this was common practice in Brazil,
where in some parishes one priest may be responsible for
as many as fifty thousand people; laypeople bury the dead,
he explained, and their pastors offer a weekly Mass commemorating all the recently deceased. In the end, the vote
was 136 to 113 against any change, the American bishops,
in essence, voting to be even more conservative on this
issue than Rome itself.

After each of the sessions, reporters buttonholed bishops who had spoken out on what appeared to be the most
newsworthy items, or sought out bishops they knew personally, who might thus be disposed to give them a statement. The Archbishop of Milwaukee, however, was not
sought out. He said little on the floor, and, not being one
of the more outspoken proponents of either the liberal or
the conservative side, his usefulness was deemed marginal
by the press. His only sustained interchange with journal-

ists came in a Monday-afternoon press conference on a
trip that he and three of the other bishops would make
later that week to El Salvador. In attendance were most
of the print reporters covering the meeting, as well as an
EWTN crew and two crews from local television stations.
Weakland began by stating the reasons for the journey:
"To show our solidarity with the people of El Salvador,
with the Jesuit community as they commemorate those
who were murdered, with our fellow-bishops in El Salvador, and with the refugees in Chalatenango province,
which we will visit." But a forthcoming trip to a Central
American country afflicted with chronic problems was less
newsworthy, as far as the reporters were concerned, than
the denial of Weakland's honorary degree from Fribourg.

Yes, Weakland acknowledged, he had criticized the tactics of the anti-abortion movement rather strongly; no, he
was not advocating abortion.

How did he read the Vatican's refusal?

After reflecting for a moment, he called it "the first test
case" of a document issued by John Paul earlier that fall
which asked Catholic universities and theological schools
to limit their dissent to Rome's teaching to "dissent in
your heart."

Was he surprised by the denial of the degree?

"Yes."

Disappointed?

"Yes. And," the Archbishop added, "if I were the president of a Catholic university I'd be a little bit nervous. I'd
be looking over my shoulder. But I think that's the role of
a bishop—to say it as you see it."

As the conference unfolded, it seemed almost as though
there were two meetings in progress—one of a few dozen

active, vocal participants and another of some two hundred and fifty men who were merely tolerating the goings on. Archbishop Daniel Pilarczyk, of Cincinnati, the N.C.C.B. president, ran the sessions with emotionless efficiency and precision, chiding the balky and untidy who sought to stray from the agenda ("Bishop, if we are to take up the Persian Gulf further, can you tell me what item or items we will cancel?"), and issuing breathtaking parliamentary pronouncements ("Am I correct, Bishop, that yours is an amendment to the amendment on the floor, which, in turn, amends the original amendment?"). The Archbishop of Milwaukee sat impassively some three or four tables back from the podium, occasionally making notes in the margins of his set of conference papers. Infrequently, his eyes would flare wide open and his eyebrows would arch, sending a gentle ripple up his forehead. As I had come to know, this was evidence less of exasperation than of an attempt to clear his mind, to force it not to wander further. He was not alone in his ennui. Archbishop Hunthausen, a slightly rumpled man who had battled the Church over more than terminology, looked tired and somewhat wistful, as if he were attending the wake of a beloved old seminary instructor who had once been instrumental in his life. Bishop Thomas Gumbleton, an auxiliary of Detroit, who had recently returned from Baghdad with some two dozen American hostages, sat reading the *National Catholic Reporter, Commonweal,* and a sheaf of position papers on hot spots in Central America and the Middle East, as if he were still upstairs in his room.

The document on inclusive language, which had gone through seven drafts by the time the conference convened, had suffered a withering assault in committee, as salvo after salvo of amendments was fired at it by concerned prelates. On the floor, the disputation continued. Could the bishops agree that "the feminine pronoun is not to be used to refer to the Person of the Holy Spirit"? Or that "discriminatory language should be eliminated from translations insofar as possible whenever it is unfaithful to the meaning of the sacred Scripture, but the text should not be altered to adjust it to contemporary concerns"? One of those who wanted "appropriate language" to be maintained was Archbishop Anthony Bevilacqua, of Philadelphia (some six months later, he and Archbishop Mahony would be elevated to the rank of cardinal), who scrutinized every jot and tittle of the document with a proofreader's diligence, his owlish eyebrows bent over dark, deep-set eyes. After a last barrage of amendments had been offered and voted down, the document was accepted. It provides guidelines for liturgical prayers and scriptural readings which will result in "fidelity to the word of God" while keeping exclusively male references to a minimum.

An uncharacteristically passionate interchange took place during the debate on the document entitled "Human Sexuality: A Catholic Perspective for Education and Lifelong Learning." The document reasserted the Church's condemnation of any means of artificial birth control—a point that disturbed men like Bishop Kenneth Untener, of Saginaw, Michigan, who seemed on the verge of tears as he proclaimed that the issue had cast the Church as "a dysfunctional family that is unable to talk openly about a problem that everyone knows is there." In a debate on a section of the document concerning "persons with a homosexual orientation," the bishops reaffirmed a 1976 pastoral letter holding that "homosexual [persons], like everyone else, should not suffer from prejudice against their basic human rights. They have a right to respect, friendship, and justice. They should have an active role in the Christian community," and noted that "such an orientation in itself, because not freely chosen, is not sinful." A bloc of the traditionalist bishops balked at this, arguing for inclusion of a document issued in 1986 by Cardinal Ratzinger's Congregation for the Doctrine of the Faith which held that "although the particular inclination of the homosexual person is not a sin, it is a more or less strong tendency ordered toward an intrinsic moral evil; and thus the inclination itself must be seen as an objective disorder." But here, in the end, the more moderate bishops prevailed, and the citation was relegated to a footnote. It was an artful compromise, soothing both the Vatican and those bishops who bridled at such pejorative language.

As I wandered about the pressroom during one excruciatingly languid segment of the debate over inclusive language, I met one of the living legends of Catholic journalism—Father Francis X. Murphy, a Redemptorist, who, as Xavier Rynne, reported in the mid-sixties on the inner workings of Vatican II for *The New Yorker*. Father Murphy is now seventy-seven, gray-haired, with a well-trimmed goatee. "The hand of Rome, my boy, the hand of Rome. That's what's happening, for God's sake! Just say it!" he huffed after I offered a rather guarded appraisal of the degree of initiative shown by America's bishops. "Rome will always try to push its own agenda. But what continually surprises me these days is why the American Church doesn't learn from other national churches. The French, the Germans, the Belgians have from time to time told the Vatican to bug off, and they have had some effect. You have to continually stand up to the guys in Rome, or they'll plow you right under. If twenty-five American bishops were to gather together and issue a statement proclaiming that they would no longer be dominated by Rome, it would be over. They would have their autonomy, instead of allowing the ecclesiastical twerps, the sycophants in their midst, to have such a disproportionate say."

I asked two people about Father Murphy's proposition. One was Bishop Raymond Lucker, of New Ulm, Minnesota, a handsome, rather ascetic-looking prelate in his mid-sixties, whom I met at a cocktail party for the press — an event intended to provide an opportunity for prelates and press to mingle informally. It featured ossified cheese and crackers that looked like they had been recycled from another, earlier function, an open bar, many reporters, and precious few bishops. Like Weakland, Bishop Lucker was appointed by Pope Paul VI and has had his difficulties with Rome in the years since.

"Why don't twenty-five of us stand up?" he replied, with a genuinely puzzled look on his face. "I honestly don't know. This is our home — we can't burn it down. This is our mother — we can't defy her. We were trained to be loyal. You don't shake that, even if you really dislike what Rome does to you personally. Somewhere — and I never knew exactly where or when, because there is no due process in these things — I offended Rome, and I continue to pay for it. Maybe it was eleven or twelve years ago, when I issued a pastoral, with another Minnesota bishop, on women's role in the Church, which made the point — very strongly — that sexism was sinful. Now, we didn't get out and wave a banner for women's ordination, or anything like that. Or maybe it's because I'm one of the few bishops belonging to the Catholic Theological Society, which asks questions that the Vatican Congregations are not always happy to hear. Whatever it was, word came to me through the grapevine that I was in disfavor, and that I was going nowhere from New Ulm. In the hierarchy, even a lateral move is considered a sign of approval, so Rome has punished me for speaking out in the most effective way it could. I was a threat to Rome; therefore, I was to be marginalized."

Lucker fell silent for a moment, gazing into the middle distance. "There is a mind-set in Rome holding that change is wrong and frightening, that to raise questions is in itself a challenge to the authority of the Pope and to the integrity of doctrine," he continued. "For those in power in Rome, the Church is not 'the people of God' that Vatican II talked about. It is an imperial monarchy that must maintain absolute control. In such a system, those in charge can exercise raw power, because their judgment is automatically correct and they need not worry about the consequences. They have to be right; that is the highest aim, good, object. And, conversely, error has no rights. So if you are deemed to be in error Rome feels that it has the duty to punish you. Withholding approval for Weakland's degree, keeping Lucker in New Ulm. That kind of stuff. Now, all that said, utterly dispassionately, what happens? How long can I be concerned only about this Church as my home, and not about the people who are being hurt by it and leaving? I ask myself that almost every day."

Another view came from Father Thomas Reese, a Jesuit whose 1989 book, *Archbishop*, is the most complete contemporary treatment of the selection and functioning of the American Catholic hierarchy. "These men, regardless of their differences, are team players," he said. "Whether or not they have any power, the mythology of the magisterium—the authentic teaching voice of the Church—must be maintained at these meetings. But can you imagine what a strain that puts on a man? To have to go through the charade of brotherhood with the only peers that you have? To lead two lives—one at home and another here? For a man like Weakland to be well accepted in his archdiocese and a respected national figure, and yet to be regarded by his superiors as a man with no judgment?"

Outside the general sessions and various committee and regional meetings, there was time for two staples of convention life: shopping, and getting away from the convention. For the bishops, the shopping was of a specialized sort. In the Shoreham's suite 340, P. J. (Pat) McDermott displayed a line of clerical clothing and vestments, offering one-stop shopping for virtually everything a bishop might need, from alb to zucchetto. Sharing the suite was Paul Sullivan, who was there to help new bishops select a design for a coat of arms, which his company would then supply. As for recreation, on Tuesday night Archbishop Weakland bowed out of his customary annual dinner with Milwaukee priests studying canon law in Washington (this year, there were only two) and instead went out to dinner with a cousin, Eric Rice, his wife, Carol, and their son, Eric, Jr., who live in the Washington area.

At the restaurant, the Archbishop noted that, had the Vatican not intervened, he would have been on a plane bound for Switzerland at that hour. His relatives joined in one toast to the Curia officials who had made the dinner possible, and another to the Archbishop for being such a "bad boy." Their openness—even their freshness—with him was remarkable. An avowed feminist, Carol told the Archbishop that she found herself hating to go to Mass, seeing only men—a priest and altar boys—before her. Talk meandered to Uncle Mugsy, the family's eccentric, and then to Eric's wait for a kidney transplant. His son had donated one of his kidneys to his father, but the father's body had rejected it. He was now on dialysis almost daily.

Other bishops were out that night, too, for pleasure or for professional reasons. When I returned to the Shoreham later in the evening, I saw one of them, a man who is among the most vocal of the young traditionalists. He was staggeringly drunk, and had a wonderful, almost beatific smile on his face, quite unlike the expression he customarily wore during the general sessions.

The vaunted executive session on Wednesday was not under the confessional seal, and within minutes of its conclusion it was not difficult to find out from any number of bishops what had gone on. There had been two significant occurrences. A stronger letter opposing United States involvement in the Persian Gulf was to be sent—over the objection of a group of bishops led informally by Cardinal Law, who maintained that men of religion should not impose their views on those enmeshed in a difficult political situation. Law's persuasiveness was limited—and, in fact, suspect—given that he had spent the previous weekend at Camp David with the letter's intended recipient. And Bishop James Malone, of Youngstown, Ohio, had requested the floor to speak on behalf of the Archbishop of Milwaukee. Malone had previously asked Weakland if he might say or do something about the Fribourg incident, and Weakland had replied that Malone might, but that he would prefer that it not take the form of any kind of statement or resolution, since this would require the issuance of a document, and the only logical recipient would be the Vatican. "You never win on those," Weakland told Malone. In the executive session, Malone said that he, and perhaps his fellow-bishops, would like to register "moral support for Rembert at this moment." The response was a sustained standing ovation.

The conference ended early on Thursday afternoon. Steinfels' analysis in the *Times* was that while America's bishops had stood up boldly against war in the Persian Gulf, their division between liberals and conservatives had confined them to "nibbling on the edges of internal troubles." The bishops had blanched at significant doctrinal changes — changes that American Catholics seemed to want, some of which were already openly or covertly practiced in certain dioceses. An enormous, yearlong effort had produced a thick volume of documents whose intended audience might well ignore them.

An arena of more tangible battles, where casualties are not simply bruised egos or stalled careers, lay before the Archbishop of Milwaukee as a TACA Airlines jet climbed into the morning sky outside Washington the following day, banked, and headed southwest, toward El Salvador. Talking about the past few days and looking ahead to El Salvador, the Archbishop was his usual forthcoming self—forthcoming, that is, once he had read his breviary, something he always does at the beginning of a flight. The psalms feed his soul and calm his nerves. Though he has flown hundreds of thousands of miles, he is still terrified of flying. He calls it the great penance of his life.

"The N.C.C.B. is a strange group," he said. "It is theological in the deepest sense, in that we, the prime teachers, come together to discern how best to lead our people. And then there is a little of the Mafia in it, too. A conspiracy of silence. Never criticize each other in public. You are not just an individual there but part of a college of bishops, and you have to take into account how what you say will affect your peers. You come away with a great sense of togetherness, but it is essentially false. We are not united, in the way a monastic community is. Back when I was at St. Vincent's abbey, we would break out the beer after a tough meeting and regroup, trying to lay aside our differences and go on. Bishops don't get that chance. We are thrown together for a few days once a year, given an enormous agenda, and expected to somehow develop a bond. We've tried informal retreats—no agenda, just spending time together. The first one, in Collegeville, Minnesota, a few years ago, seemed to break down some barriers; you could begin to relate as human beings rather than as Church executives. But then for the second, in Santa Clara, some of the key players—like Law, and O'Connor, and Archbishop Francis Stafford, of Denver—didn't attend, and Roger Mahony just dropped in briefly, so there was really no point to it.

"If I were the N.C.C.B. president looking out over the assembly, I think I would have a profound feeling that these men do not have their hearts in it—that they want to go home and run their dioceses as they darn well please. And why not? You quickly learn that these public meetings are not the place to make policy. You make policy at home, quietly. You try to move things there, not in Washington. If I can ever get the third section of my pastoral letter on the priesthood together, I think that it might serve as a good example. For some of the bishops who have spent no time in Rome, there is a mystique about the place, and during these national meetings they tend to fall back on Rome in matters of theology. 'Will Rome be pleased?' they ask themselves. I spent thirteen years in Rome; the Vatican is demythologized for me. It is not the repository of truth and right thinking that some make it out to be—not at all. I know what happens in the back rooms there, so, frankly, I spend little time forecasting what Rome may think. But I have to hand it to the Vati-

can. It has been successful; it has sent a chill through the
American Church. Take Hunthausen – Dutch, we call him.
Rome broke him, and the point was made that anyone
who follows in his footsteps will be similarly broken. The
implied message is 'If you stand up to us, you're going to
suffer.' " (Archbishop Hunthausen later announced that
he would leave office in August, on his seventieth birthday,
five years before his mandatory retirement date.)

Weakland ordered a bourbon before lunch. Afterward,
as we sipped our coffee, I asked him about loneliness,
which is often mentioned as a reason so many priests are
leaving clerical life. How much more of a problem is it for
a bishop, who sees his peers only a few days a year and
then spends most of his hours with them in formal meetings?

"Loneliness is an easy way of talking about it," he
answered. "It really comes down to celibacy, don't you
think? The trick in dealing with celibacy is to understand
that there is no true substitute for the intimacy of marriage. We were taught that the Divine Office, your community, your prayer life were substitutes, but they are not.
Travel, an intellectual life, and, in the case of a bishop, a
measure of authority, power: these are not substitutes,
either. I'm over sixty – for me, it's not about sex. When it
hits me hardest is not when I'm in trouble or want to pour
my heart out because I'm depressed. It's when I have a
great idea that I'd like to share with someone, when I've
heard a new piece of music and want someone to sit down
and listen with me. My trip to Russia last summer: I have
no one – nobody on the same wavelength – with whom I
can talk about what I saw, what I felt. That's a burden I
have to live with. While I see the great merit in celibacy –

the freedom it gives you—perhaps there are people who can't make that sacrifice. And yet we continue to demand that they do—if they want to be priests. Across-the-board celibacy works to our detriment as a Church.

"Men who leave the priesthood because of the loneliness are not weak. They are simply good men who have fallen in love with good women. If we are alive, we are continually falling in love. You asked me once if I had ever fallen in love. Yes—at twelve, and most recently at sixty-four. I'm falling in love all the time. When I was in my forties, the women I found attractive were usually twenty years younger. Now that's changed; age means nothing. I find intelligent women, whatever their age, extraordinarily enticing—intelligent women who are not afraid of me, who are interested in me as me, and not because I'm well known. But I am aware of when I'm falling in love. It's dangerous ever to think that all that is over with—that you won't fall in love again. I have to be on guard not to let my emotions run away, not to make excuses to see someone who has set off the spark. So far, I've done pretty well."

Our discussion at an end, and El Salvador closer than Washington, the Archbishop took up a novel (one of Jon Hassler's depictions of Midwestern Catholicism), and later, in the final hour of the flight, managed a brief nap. As the senior prelate, he was heading the ten-person delegation, which included, besides the three bishops—Walter Sullivan, of Richmond; Ricardo Ramirez, of Las Cruces; and Carlos Sevilla, an auxiliary from San Francisco—two priests, a nun, a lay worker, and Eileen Purcell and Oscar Chacon, who work for SHARE, the Salvadoran Humanitarian Aid, Research, and Education Foundation, which organized the visit. Recent events, both in El Salvador and in the United States, had conspired to make this a crucial time in the ten-year-old war between the Salvadoran government and the Farabundo Martí National Liberation Front—the F.M.L.N. The pretrial judicial investigation into the brutal murder, the year before, of six Jesuits, their housekeeper, and the housekeeper's daughter by Salvadoran Army soldiers was dragging on and on, and the murders and the ineffective investigation had severely eroded support in the United States Congress for the government of President Alfredo Cristiani; indeed, barely a month earlier Congress had made the first significant cut in military aid to El Salvador. Negotiations between the Salvadoran government and the F.M.L.N., begun during the summer, had stalled, and both sides had resorted to their old tactics. The F.M.L.N. was threatening another major offensive, randomly attacking Army units; its mortar attacks on power pylons were causing unnerving blackouts in one part of El Salvador or another almost every night. Meanwhile, the Army was stepping up its own terror campaign: mutilated bodies were again being found, and suspected F.M.L.N. sympathizers were disappearing. The offices of newspapers and human-rights groups were being ransacked or bombed; people living in rural areas thought to be F.M.L.N. refuges were being subjected to harassment by the military.

At a late-afternoon briefing at Catholic University the day before the delegation left Washington, Weakland had listened pensively as Ms. Purcell—an intense, dark-haired woman in her thirties, who was SHARE's executive director—gave the delegation a rapid-fire summation of what they could expect: "This is a country at war. Fighting can break out at any time, any place. If you find yourself in the middle of a combat area, hit the ground. Wait for word to stand up. Do not go out on the streets alone, even in daylight. Stay with the group. Realize that any telephone you use could be tapped. We will be going into Chalatenango province, in the north, to visit Father Jon de Cortina and some of the resettlement areas there. This has been the scene of some of the worst fighting over the years. I think all of you are aware that Father Cortina was shot at just a few months ago. I don't think anything will happen. If anything did happen to four American bishops, the outcry would be more than the present government would want to face. Largely because of the Jesuits' murder, American support for the government is slipping, and the country's leaders know it. In a way, they have to let us in. But we are suspect, because we will be going into conflict areas — areas controlled by the F.M.L.N. We will be stopped at military checkpoints. We may be searched. The military will make it as hard as they can for us to move about. The government doesn't want us to come, and some elements of the Salvadoran Church would be happier if we stayed home. But the people want us. Just so you know. And," she added, "if you are arrested, try to stay calm. We'll find you; you won't be detained long."

As the abbot primate of the Benedictines from 1967 to 1977, Weakland had visited monasteries in many countries, but he had gone into a combat area only once before — in 1968, when he visited Saigon and Hue. While he did not welcome the thought of doing so again, he knew that this was a visit long overdue. Milwaukee parishes supported the work of Father Cortina in Chalatenango, and he felt that he needed to demonstrate his backing for that work. And there was still another, more personal reason. In the early 1980s, when the Milwaukee archdiocese offered sanctuary for refugees fleeing the war in El Salvador, Weakland took a Salvadoran couple, Felix and Norma (they used no last name for fear of reprisals at home), and their children into a house adjoining the cathedral rectory. "It was soon obvious they were people who had witnessed unspeakable suffering, torture, and violence," he recalled. "One of the girls was eight when a soldier came into her classroom and impaled her teacher on his bayonet. And yet the faith of the family was at such a deep level—not a catechized faith, but so, so strong and real for them. El Salvador was just a name before then for me. They evangelized me about their country." As he went to bed in a simply furnished Catholic University dormitory room the night before the trip and slept the few, fitful hours before an early morning wake-up call, the Archbishop realized that he was at a minimum apprehensive, and, when he thought about it further, actually afraid.

Although SHARE had tried twice before to bring Weakland to El Salvador, the trips had been cancelled at the last moment because the political situation had become too volatile. But now, with a commemorative Mass scheduled to mark the first anniversary of the Jesuits' deaths, priests and bishops from many countries were converging on San Salvador, and the government had little choice but to grant entry to the SHARE delegation. Ms. Purcell correctly calculated that it was not in the government's interest to refuse permission to one of the largest contingents of bishops ever to visit El Salvador from the country that had provided more than four billion dollars in economic and military aid in the previous ten years.

Because she had a group of high-level American church-men to offer, high-level meetings had been arranged: one with President Cristiani; another with Colonel René Emilio Ponce, the Defense Minister; and a third with the American Ambassador, William Walker. A clandestine meeting with the F.M.L.N., while not on the itinerary, was a possibility.

What Weakland and his fellow-bishops hoped to impart to each side in the tragic war—which had by then claimed perhaps seventy-five thousand military and civilian lives—was the urgent need to resume peace negotiations. And the trip had a second, equally important purpose—one that only men of their ecclesiastical stature could hope to accomplish. While El Salvador is a country with a strong Roman Catholic tradition—ninety per cent of the people are at least nominal Catholics—the Church is having an extraordinarily difficult time maintaining its credibility there. Over the past decade, as openings for bishops occurred, the Vatican had appointed men of neutral or pro-government sentiment; in effect, it was sending a message to those in El Salvador who favor an activist social gospel—a gospel that would necessarily overturn the financial hegemony held by a dozen or so families and maintained by the military—that the Church was to be neither a staging point for revolutionary activities nor a haven for those involved in the struggle. Basically, the Church in El Salvador was to get out of politics and back to saving souls.

Though the Salvadoran Church is probably best known as the Church of Archbishop Oscar Romero, who was murdered in March of 1980 for speaking forthrightly about the needs of his country's poor and their oppression by the oligarchy and the government, it has largely not carried on in Romero's tradition. The allegiance of most of its bishops is to the Pope and the Church, and not to a national movement. (Central America's only cardinal — Miguel Obando y Bravo, of Nicaragua — is a man less than sympathetic to revolutionary movements in the region and to the liberation theology that fuels them.) While the circumstances in which the American Church finds itself are much less dire, Weakland recognized the similarity of the response from the Vatican: bishops and cardinals in the United States, too, were being chosen for their orthodoxy and their loyalty to Rome, and he had consistently maintained that the Church was the poorer for it. A major reason for his visit was to show his support for Archbishop Arturo Rivera y Damas, who succeeded Romero, and who has continued to speak out against the carnage and the economic inequities.

PART III

❧ EL SALVADOR ☙

Our arrival at the San Salvador airport, early on a steamy afternoon, went without a hitch; the only sign of the military was a single soldier, in full battle dress, with an American-made M-16 cradled in his palm and a look of boredom on his face, who paid no attention to us as immigration officials perfunctorily checked our passports and visas. We were then driven to Centro Loyola, a Jesuit retreat house and conference center nestled in the foothills on the outskirts of the city, where most of our delegation would be lodged.

Four hours later, we joined the other clerical delegations, at the Universidad Centroamericana. In a large assembly hall behind the university chapel—a chapel where the six Jesuits had often said Mass, and where they are now buried—some two hundred priests (many of them Jesuits) and fourteen bishops and archbishops vested for a memorial Mass. Almost all wore red stoles over their white albs, and the hall was thick with daubs of dazzling color as the men moved about—a scene reminiscent of the concelebrated Mass at the bishops' conference in Washington, except that here the color stood not for the primacy of office but for the sacrifice of martyrs' blood.

The mood was hardly sombre, however; many old friends renewed acquaintance, and when Archbishop

Rivera y Damas arrived, Weakland greeted him with a warm *abrazo* and spoke to him in passable Spanish. Rivera y Damas, a handsome, stately man with jet-black hair and olive skin, said little in return; he seemed overwhelmed by the roomful of fellow-clerics. "He invited no one from abroad," Weakland told me, as we stood to one side and watched others greet the Archbishop of San Salvador. "But you can see he's happy that so many came. It must be hard for him to live up to their expectations. Will he be another Romero? Does he want to be?"

The politics of religion in El Salvador was quickly apparent as the members of the hierarchy took their places on an enormous outdoor stage. El Salvador has eleven bishops, but only three in addition to Rivera y Damas were present: Eduardo Alas, of Chalatenango; Rodrigo Orlando Cabrera-Cuellar, of Santiago de Maria; and the San Salvador auxiliary, Gregorio Rosa y Chavez. When Archbishop Weakland asked Rivera y Damas about this later, he said, "I don't know—they may have been afraid they would be booed when they were introduced." Immediately after the murder of the Jesuits, Rivera y Damas had pointed to the military as culpable. Other Salvadoran bishops had criticized him for what they considered a rash judgment, and had flown off to Rome—reputedly at the government's expense—to repeat their complaints to the Pope.

In front of the elevated altar, a crowd of three or four thousand spilled out across a broad field at the center of the campus. Hundreds of people from Chalatenango, the country's northernmost province, had arrived the day before and had slept overnight on the grass. "The Jesuits spent much time in the villages of Chalatenango," one of the local priests told me. "In one way or another, all these people knew them."

As the Mass got under way, a night breeze began to rustle the leaves of the tall eucalyptus trees ringing the field, but it was still quite hot, and the celebrants perspired beneath their vestments. At the offertory, eight small apothecary jars were brought to the stage and set on the altar, each labelled with the name of one of the victims: Elba Ramos; Celina Ramos; Fathers Amando López Quintana, Ignacio Ellacuría, Juan Ramón Moreno Pardo, Ignacio Martín-Baró, Segundo Montes Mozo, and Joaquín López y López. Within the jars were soil, dried grass, twigs, and other matter soaked with blood, which had been collected from the site after the bodies were removed. Archbishop Weakland—a man who prides himself on keeping his emotions in check—was startled to find that his body was covered with gooseflesh.

The next day, after a morning spent at the joint military high command tediously duplicating paperwork that had already been filled out in order to obtain a *salvaconducto*, the delegation set out on the Via Dolorosa that Church people who come to El Salvador customarily take. The most recent additions to the tour—which grows longer with the years and the deaths—are a walk through the Jesuits' residence, a visit to a small museum beside the chapel, and, finally, a stop at a grassy area behind the residence, where most of the bodies were found. Father Jesus Sariego, the Jesuits' local director of religious formation, recounted the events of the night of November 16, 1989, in a voice so measured and lacking in any trace of the maudlin that he might have been describing an exhibit of pre-Columbian art. Soldiers had massed on the edge of the U.C.A. campus that night, he told us, and had shot into the air, simulating a pitched battle with F.M.L.N. guerrillas, who had launched an audacious offensive in San Salvador a few days before. It was a moonless night, and in the darkness about seventy troops divided into two units and moved on the residence. Some battered on the front door — a sturdy one, made of metal — and one of the Jesuits eventually opened it, imploring the troops not to destroy it. The other group negotiated a network of paths and passageways between campus buildings (a route of such intricacy that it indicated that the operation had been well planned and practiced), scaled a fence, and approached the residence from the rear.

The two women, Elba and Celina Ramos, were killed first. Ironically, they had been spending the night there for safety. The soldiers shot both of them in the head and then put their M-16s under the women's dresses and virtually disembowelled them. Five of the priests were marched or dragged outside, and there they were shot. The sixth — Father López y López — hid under his bed, and was killed on the spot as soon as he was found. Photographs in the museum depict the violence of the slaughter — Father Ellacuría's brain is on the grass, eight inches from his head — and also a certain serenity. Father Martín-Baró's legs are crossed at the ankles, in relaxed fashion. He was killed with a single bullet to the head, and Father Sariego conjectured that he had waited for his death patiently. A Bible had been cut nearly in two by a burst from an automatic rifle. A picture of Oscar Romero had been perforated by a bullet; another was scorched by an incendiary white phosphorus, and the frame had melted, forming two long plastic teardrops on either side of Romero's face, which was almost obliterated.

Beside a roped-off area in back of the residence, where six red and two yellow rosebushes commemorate the deaths, Archbishop Weakland led a short prayer for peace in El Salvador. As the group was leaving, he fell in step with Oscar Chacon. "Why would they do it?" Oscar asked, repeating a question from another member of the group. "And why like this? By blowing their brains out, the military were trying to kill the priests' ideas. These were the most visible members of the Jesuit community, and by killing them the military was saying to anyone who opposes it, 'We can kill you, too.' " Archbishop Weakland nodded. Oscar, a soft-spoken young man, is a native Salvadoran, and he had seen many of his childhood friends killed in the past decade. When he thought that the four prelates were out of earshot, he said to me, "So much of it is psychological. You never know when or how you might get it. Basically, the government's message was 'Don't fuck with us or you're dead.' "

Later that afternoon, the delegation was taken to Archbishop Romero's tomb, in El Salvador's National Cathedral. The sarcophagus was covered with dozens of small marble plaques attesting to miraculous favors granted to those who had prayed to Romero. As daylight faded, we drove across town to the Carmelite Chapel of the Hospital of the Divine Providence, where Romero was killed. A single .22-calibre bullet fired through the open chapel doors from a parked car some two hundred yards away had pierced Romero's heart. One of the Carmelite nuns escorted us through Romero's home, a simple three-room cottage nearby. In a glass-enclosed closet was the alb he was wearing when he said his last Mass; his blood had dried into long dull-brown streaks on the white poplin garment.

As we were getting ready to leave, the lights in the Carmelite convent flickered and went out. Blackouts had become a nightly occurrence, and the nuns carried flashlights as matter-of-factly as they wore their rosaries. The air was suddenly thick with the sound of helicopters. They were unmistakably close, but we couldn't see them; they were flying low, behind the trees, and presumably without lights. Oscar had heard on the clandestine F.M.L.N. radio station that there had been military activity in the south and east of the country. Forty-eight casualties had been reported—a tally whose accuracy Oscar said could not be trusted but which did indicate that extended combat had taken place. In the distance, on the outskirts of the capital, came the sporadic, muffled thuds of mortars exploding. The F.M.L.N. offensive appeared to have begun, and that night's sleep for the Archbishop was even more fitful than it had been on the eve of the trip.

The next day was Sunday, and that morning Weakland, Sullivan, Ramirez, and Sevilla concelebrated the eight-o'clock Mass with Archbishop Rivera y Damas at the Basilica of the Sacred Heart, in downtown San Salvador. It was this Mass that had formed the cornerstone of Romero's ministry, since it was the one place where an accurate portrayal of the week's events and the government's activities could be given uncensored. Romero's sermons at the eight-o'clock Mass had, in effect, signed his death warrant. Six weeks before his assassination, in a talk at the University of Louvain, in Belgium, entitled "The Political Dimension of Faith," Romero summed up what he had been saying week after week in San Salvador: "Christian faith does not separate us from the world but, rather, submerges us in it. The Church is not an élite but, rather, a follower of that Jesus who lived, worked, struggled, and died in the midst of the city. When the Church inserts herself in the sociopolitical world in order to cooperate in bringing about the emergence of life for the poor, she is not undertaking a mere subsidiary task, or something outside her mission, but is witnessing to her faith in God, and is being an instrument of the Spirit, Lord and Giver of Life."

As they moved in procession down the main aisle of the basilica, Weakland and the other American bishops were surprised to see several local television camera crews set up in front of the Communion rail. Print and radio journalists stood ready with their tape recorders to record the sermon, which was to be given by the San Salvador auxiliary, Rosa y Chavez. The auxiliary bishop's sermon proved an interesting combination of indignation and prudence, by a man who had come to office as a political and theological conservative—the Vatican's hoped-for antidote to Rivera y Damas—and then had been profoundly shaken by the Jesuits' deaths. This morning, although condemning the violence against the Jesuits and the ineffectual investigation of their murders, Rosa y Chavez noted that "we did not agree with everything the Jesuits did"—an apparent allusion to their contacts with the F.M.L.N. and their work in pro-rebel villages. Most of the members of the delegation who understood Spanish were distressed at this, and so when the press corps asked for a post-Mass press conference Weakland quickly agreed. The journalists, however, asked a series of rather anodyne questions: reasons for the visit, impressions of El Salvador, and so forth. They had heard that a meeting with President Cristiani was scheduled for the following Tuesday. What would the visitors be telling Cristiani?

Weakland knew that his remarks would reach the Presidential palace before he did. "Surely, we will say that the talks must continue between the government and the F.M.L.N., and the murders must be solved," he said. "But all of that could have been said before we came here. We will know better what to say to the President after we talk to the people—after our trip to Chalatenango, which begins today." The Archbishop was advocating peace, and he was also—by putting the trip on the record—taking out some term insurance on his life.

Before our departure for Chalatenango, we paid a visit to Monsignor Ricardo Urioste, the vicar-general of the San Salvador archdiocese and pastor of San José Calle Real. The parish, partially supported by SHARE, is in a poor neighborhood on the outskirts of the city, and provides basic medical care to some twenty-two thousand people; there are no other medical facilities in the area. Shortly before noon, all of us except for Bishop Sevilla, who was to fly on to Guatemala the next day, boarded a van for the trip north. The road was paved only as far as the provincial capital; we would be driven there in the van and then switch to rough-terrain vehicles.

As Eileen Purcell had anticipated, the drive went slowly. The province was only about fifty kilometres north of San Salvador, but the trip took the rest of the day. At each of four checkpoints—heralded by speed bumps and fortified with sandbags, some of which had been in place so long that they were sprouting weeds—soldiers with blank, hard faces that belied their youth swaggered toward us in deliberate slow motion, checked our documents, and made what were probably simulated calls to the military high command. Their palpable suspicion of the three prelates bordered on disgust. The bishops, who were used to

at least a modicum of deference and respect, found themselves abruptly recast as meddling do-gooders—those who
aid the enemy and make the war even more difficult to
fight.

When we arrived in the provincial capital—a town of
some twenty-eight thousand, named after the province but
popularly known as Chalate—Bishop Alas was waiting for
us in his chancery, which was no more than a few rooms
in a small attached house on one of the streets leading to
the center. Alas took us a few doors down to a local restaurant, where we had a huge lunch of fried plantains,
chicken, tortillas, and beans. Then we climbed into four-
wheel-drive Toyotas and set off on a cobblestone road to
the north, only to find that it ended abruptly just outside
Chalate's business district. The track that lay beyond was
impassable to all but pedestrians, mules, or the sturdiest
of vehicles. In the years before rebel troops took to the
mountains here, the road was well-kept enough to carry
ordinary cars and buses. It had since been allowed to dete-
riorate into a roiling stew of upended rocks, washed out
by the torrential rains that fall half the year. A road in
this condition is both a tactic and a political statement:
this road led to F.M.L.N.-controlled El Salvador; the government's aim was to deny the rebels and their civilian
supporters easy movement within the province or to its
capital, whose Army barracks the F.M.L.N. periodically
assaulted.

As the roadway tossed us about like so many rag dolls,
Archbishop Weakland, in the lead Toyota, listened attentively to Alas, who was doing the driving. Alas is a short
man with thick, curly hair who seems to be constantly smiling—though on closer scrutiny, what initially appear to be

smile lines about his eyes and mouth take strange detours. It could be from no more than years of squinting at the sun; but I read pain. Later I found that Alas is a diabetic with a stomach so temperamental that he eats mainly boiled, unseasoned vegetables. "I know what a hardship this is, but we feel your shoulder beneath our burden," Alas said to him, in Spanish. "It is bad here. If you say you are from Chalatenango, you are automatically a guerrilla. If you are a Christian, you are a guerrilla. Many of the people here had to flee the bombs, and in the process they lost their identification papers. They go to the government, and the government says it has no record of them. They cannot vote, they cannot move about, because if they move about without identification they are considered guerrillas and they are shot. Or they disappear. And these soldiers — ahh." He sighed, and tightened his grip on the wheel. "I gave many of them their first Communion. Humble boys, good boys. And now they are taught to be dominant over their own people. A woman goes to market in Chalate and brings back a pound of fish for her family and a pound for her sister, and the soldiers confiscate the fish, saying it is intended for the guerrillas. We cannot bring in batteries. Or medical supplies. The suspicion is that everything goes to the guerrillas. So where can the people turn? Only to the Church — only the Church remains. But priests are killed. I am threatened all the time. And the people wonder if the Church stands with them. *Muy, muy malo.*"

Our objective, reached after an exhausting hour-and-a-half ride, just as the sun was setting behind a mountain ridge, was a village once called Corral de Piedra and recently renamed Comunidad Ignacio Ellacuría, in com-

memoration of one of the murdered Jesuits. The delegation was greeted by a throng of campesinos, their barefoot
children, many dogs, several ducks, a pig or two, and a
priest, Father Jon de Cortina. Father Cortina was beaming
as the members of the delegation disembarked and
attempted to brush the road dust from their clothing. A
thin, angular man with fine features bespeaking an aris-
tocratic Spanish lineage, he was the head of the Engi-
neering Department at U.C.A. On the night of the
massacre he was in Chalatenango doing parish work, and
so he was spared. He subsequently decided to carry on his
priesthood principally by living and working with the province's poor rather than by teaching U.C.A. students —
young Salvadorans who are tired of the ongoing conflict,
are largely politically conservative, and tend to back the
government.

Because we were so late arriving, Father Cortina had
completed the first part of a community Mass, but while
it was still light he and his parishioners were eager to take
the *Norteamericanos* in hand and lead them to Comunidad
Ellacuría's Station of the Cross on the Salvadoran Via
Dolorosa.

The village, like the others in the area, is poor. Most of
the peasants live in mud huts with thatched roofs. And so,
nine months before on the afternoon of February 11, 1990,
as government mortars began falling on the outskirts, her-
alding yet another ground assault to flush out the
F.M.L.N., some of the residents ran for protection to a
small brick building used for grinding corn. They were
seen by the crew of a helicopter gunship. Although the
ground commander radioed the gunship that no F.M.L.N.
had been found, the gunship hovered over the building

and, once the people were inside, blasted it with machine-gun and rocket fire. One man and four children were killed, including eleven-year-old Isabel and two-year-old Vilma Beatrice, daughters of Maria Lopez.

The building had been cleared of rubble, but it had not been repaired. The inner surface of the wall that was least damaged had been smoothly plastered, and a mural had been painted on it, depicting the helicopter, guns ablaze, swooping down against the backdrop of an orange ball of sun. Bouquets of wilted flowers lay at its base. Archbishop Weakland gazed at the mural in silence. As we stood on the spot where children had huddled screaming at the deafening explosions and praying for their lives, I found my thoughts drifting back to the Children's Mass that the Archbishop had offered on a serene October morning at Our Lady Queen of Peace, in Milwaukee. There, in a majestic church, children had recited an Our Father, in firm, confident voices; here children had crouched on a dirt floor and uttered frightened pleas that for some went unanswered.

At dusk, the American clerics vested and, together with Father Cortina and the villagers, marched in a silent torch-light procession around the village perimeter, and then to a low wooden building with a corrugated-tin roof. This was the village hall, church, and gathering spot, and there the Mass resumed. At the offertory, Maria Lopez brought to the altar two plastic bags containing clothes that her daughters had once worn. She then held out her arms, offering her youngest child, with whom she had been pregnant at the time of the attack. "You can kill us, but we do not die," she said. "New life will always spring up." The baby had been named Vilma Isabel, in memory of her sisters. As I looked about me, I could see dozens upon dozens of young children, many women, and some old men, but no men between the ages of fourteen and fifty — at least, none who were not physically impaired. Only when the village was enveloped in darkness did young men emerge from the shadows of the mud huts and the surrounding jungle. Young, sound men in a village such as Comunidad Ellacuría know that they can be shot on sight.

At the conclusion of the Mass, the president of the village council read a list of the names of villagers who had died at the hands of the military. It was a litany not unlike the list of the Church's early martyrs in the Mass — a recitation so familiar that many Catholics hardly hear it. In the Mass, it is Linus, Cletus, Clement, Sixtus, Cornelius, Cyprian, Lawrence, Chrysogonus. Here it was Ananabal, Blanca Linda, Dolores, Isabel, Vilma Beatrice.

We were invited to one of the houses in the village for a supper of pasta, tortillas, and refried beans. The meal was served on the veranda, at a long table, and while we ate — by the light of a candle held by a young boy — Father Cortina told us about his ambush, and about the peace march into Chalate that may have provoked it. Some two thousand campesinos had gone with him, and when they reached the city the military forced all the residents and merchants to bolt their doors. "There we were, out in the open, no place to go, surrounded by the soldiers," Father Cortina said. "They had guns. We were chanting 'We want peace.' Perhaps it was foolish, but we cannot just sit here — nothing would change if we did. In El Salvador, to be a committed Christian is not allowed. To seek justice for those who are abused and murdered, to try to provide food for the hungry and medicine for the sick — this is consid-

ered subversive, political, because if you try to help the
poor you are automatically in opposition to the government. It's very dangerous just to have a picture of Romero
on your wall or a Bible in your house."

"Funny, isn't it?" Archbishop Weakland said. "The
Vatican always understood the political dimension of faith
in Poland, but—"

"Not down here," they said in unison, and laughed.

"So what we do," Father Cortina continued, "is work
in tiny ways, so that these people are not forgotten. It is
not about politics, or liberation theology, for goodness'
sake! It is just being the Church. That is why it means so
much that you are here. You are a sign of the Church—a
sign that we are not alone, forgotten. Salvadoran bishops
don't come here, but you have come." Father Cortina lit
a cigarette. He smokes more than two packs a day. "I could
die so easily that I'm not worried about this," he will usually say when he is advised to quit.

We drove to the village of Guarjila, five kilometres
away, to spend the night in Father Cortina's residence, a
two-room cinder-block building about twenty by thirty
feet, with a tin roof and a concrete floor—luxurious
accommodations, by Guarjila standards. Thin mattresses
were arranged on the floor of the larger room for all the
visitors except Archbishop Weakland, who, as the senior
prelate, was given an aluminum cot in Father Cortina's
room. As we were getting ready to go to bed—something
that required little preparation, since most of us would be
sleeping in our clothes—Father Cortina stamped the heel
of his sandal on the floor near the front door, then non-
chalantly kicked a huge dead scorpion outside. "They usually come in twos," he remarked, and the Americans

looked warily about them. Just then, as the Archbishop leaned against the doorjamb, something fell onto the front of his shirt, and he flicked it off. Stepping forward, Father Cortina ground a second scorpion into the floor. Few of us were relieved, however.

The first stop the next morning was San Antonio los Ranchos, a village that had been abandoned nine years earlier by its six thousand residents after the government effectively levelled it and burned the surrounding countryside in order to deny the F.M.L.N. cover and food. The jungle has since reclaimed the hillsides, which are again verdant and overgrown; and the village has been resettled by about twelve hundred of its former residents, many of whom had fled across the border to Honduras. The church in San Antonio los Ranchos — once an elegant white adobe building in the Spanish-colonial style — was the village's most substantial structure, and had served as a refuge during bombings and strafings. The façade was still intact. Archbishop Weakland walked through the portico and back into brilliant sunshine, in what had once been the narthex of the church. Stubby fluted bases marked the spots where stone columns once rose to support the ceiling. Children climbed the pocked and crumbling walls and watched us, wide grins on their faces. Father Cortina showed us a piece of steel shrapnel that had been recovered after a bombing run. It weighed about forty pounds, and was five feet long, about eight inches wide, and two inches thick, with one edge sharpened; it looked much like the blade of a giant rotary lawnmower. Some of the dozens of teeth on the other edge had broken off, as they are designed to do while the steel blade whirls about after the bomb explodes. Each tooth, travelling at high velocity on its random path, can easily kill.

One of the villages the delegation visited, little different in appearance from a number of others we saw, must remain nameless. We had been there about an hour and were sitting in the shade drinking lukewarm Cokes when a man in a white T-shirt, carrying an M-16, strode across the plaza toward a row of low buildings on the far side. This was not the arrogant saunter of a government soldier; the man's movements were at once cautious and relaxed. Once we had seen him, we began to make out more people in the shadow of the buildings that fronted on the plaza. There were men and women, carrying M-16s and Russian-made AK-47s; ammunition belts were strung over their shoulders and around their waists. Most wore dark-brown, khaki, or black shirts and trousers. (Because it is a hall-mark of the F.M.L.N., as well as effective camouflage for night patrols, black cloth cannot be sold in Chalatenango province.) The message had somehow been transmitted that the bishops wanted to hear all sides during their mission of peace and solidarity and would not refuse a meeting with the F.M.L.N.

The meeting took place in a small room overlooking the square. A young man with a machine gun resting across his knees sat outside the door, and, inside, the Archbishop of Milwaukee sat down across the table from an F.M.L.N. commandante. Bishops Ramirez and Sullivan sat on either side of Weakland; the rest of us waited in the shade on the concrete veranda of a nearby house.

"I immediately noticed three things about him," Arch-bishop Weakland told me later. "When we shook hands, his were not those of a peasant, but soft hands, with long fingers and clean, trimmed nails, and when he looked at me there was no trace of cockiness about him. He spoke perfect, cultivated Spanish. He gave me his nom de guerre and apologized immediately for not telling me his real name. I sensed early that this was not going to be a Marxist-Leninist lecture. Yet he was extremely idealistic; he reminded me of Benedictine novices I have known who have such good hearts and think the world should be perfect. He wanted a better life for the people, but he was in no way trying to convince me that what he was doing was right. He knew that it was, for him. That came through strongly. But there was a pronounced melancholy about him; this was not the life he would have chosen for himself. You can tell when people reject each other's ideas, and that didn't happen here. What he needed was a sounding board, someone who would not judge him or comment on what he was saying but just let him talk, so that he could hear himself. In that way, I guess I'd have to call it a pastoral visit. He made the point more than once that the Church is not their enemy; many of his men are Catholic. He never asked me to try to stop the American aid that goes to the government forces he fights. There seemed to be little to talk about in the present, so I asked him if the F.M.L.N. would be part of the political system once the war was over. And he said, 'That is the great question.' "

The meeting had taken no more than a half hour, and soon we were bouncing about in the Toyotas, on the bumpy ride back to Chalate. We decided to stretch our legs there before resuming our journey south, so a group of us walked around the town and past the Army barracks, which dominates Chalate's principal square. It was heavily fortified and covered with camouflage paint. A few soldiers disconsolately stood guard at the entrance, and the watchtowers were manned; there was no other sign of life, and the complex had the air of a forgotten outpost. We later heard that four hours after we left Chalate the barracks was attacked by F.M.L.N. mortar fire. The attack was followed by a pitched battle in the streets, in which eleven civilians were reported to have been killed.

T he remainder of the trip back to San Salvador, thanks to the perfunctory nature of the military checks in this direction, took only a third as long as the journey north. Before leaving Chalatenango, we made a stop at a vast cemetery on the outskirts of Chalate, in order to visit the graves of Sister Ita Ford and Sister Maura Clarke, two Maryknoll nuns who, along with a lay worker from Cleveland named Jean Donovan and an Ursuline nun, Sister Dorothy Kazel, were murdered by Salvadoran troops in 1980. Their murderers have never been tried. As we drove on into the city, Bishop Sullivan leaned over to Archbishop Weakland and patted his arm. "Rembert, hard to realize that just a couple of days ago we were honestly spending a lot of time debating whether to use 'person' instead of 'man,' or whether laypeople should be allowed to preside at funerals," he said. "Isn't that something?"

Weakland put his hand on Sullivan's. "I honestly don't give a damn what words we're supposed to use," he said. "Or who says them, or who votes for what. Get the poor souls in the ground, and say some prayers over them, that's what matters."

The dust of the road had permeated the interior of our vehicles again, and by the time we had worked our way through the evening rush-hour traffic and back to Centro Loyola we were a scruffy lot. After showering, we went to dinner at Doña Mercedes, a pleasant and spacious restaurant on the Boulevard los Héroes, and relived the experience of what had seemed like weeks but was in fact only two days. The trip had forged a camaraderie among the group—except, it appeared, for one member. The Archbishop seemed out of his element now; he sat off by himself at the corner of the bar, dressed far too warmly in a white-and-gray patterned sweater, and sipping a drink. This sudden distancing seemed to reflect something profound about Weakland's character. In the course of his personal and professional formation, he had been either intensely alone or intensely in community with a self-selected few. He had entered the monastic life as a boy of thirteen, and in his thirties he had begun his rise to positions of greater and greater authority, from which there had been no descent. He did not seem at ease here, where there was no agenda, no particular reason for all of us to be together. We were not his family, or his real friends; we were not the brother monks he knew so well. He seemed not so much lost in his own world as tentative about entering ours; I sensed that he didn't know exactly what to do or say, or how to act. Or was this perhaps the moody man he had spoken of back in Milwaukee—the man unsure of himself, feeling unequal to the task that lay ahead the next day?

During dinner, the conversation turned to the coming meetings with President Cristiani, Colonel Ponce, and Ambassador Walker, and the Archbishop seemed to come back to himself, the next day's possibilities now enlivening him. "We have a limited amount of time," he announced.

"We have to take control of it quickly, or else we'll just be lectured to. That's what the Pope does. When you pay him a visit, you'd better have an agenda. Jon Cortina must be protected. The government must help those people in the north — at least, stop persecuting them. The Army has to be scaled back if any lasting peace is to come and any money is to be made available to address the awful poverty. The investigation into the Jesuits' death — the government has to know that American sentiment is changing very quickly."

The next morning, en route to the meetings with the President and the Defense Minister, the Archbishop and his delegation ran a gantlet of armed guards, ranging from uniformed soldiers with automatic rifles at the front gate of the Presidential palace to a young man straddling the hood of a Chevrolet parked near the palace steps, who wore a glove of woven metal bristling with studs. It was a gantlet run for a small prize: we were met not by President Cristiani or Defense Minister Ponce but by Cristiani's chief of staff, Ernesto Altschul, who is frequently quoted as a spokesman for the Salvadoran government. Altschul, who wore a well-tailored tropical-weight suit and spoke in nearly unaccented English, apologized for the absence of the country's leaders, explaining that they were in "urgent meetings" because of the F.M.L.N. offensive. He quickly made the delegation aware of his credentials for this occasion: he had been educated by Jesuits at Loyola University in New Orleans, he had been married by Oscar Romero, and he had taken an eighty-per-cent pay cut in leaving private industry for government work. He listened with a serious but somewhat practiced air as Archbishop Weakland decried the deaths of innocent civilians in the north,

Father Cortina's ambush, and the ongoing persecution of the Church. The government's assaults, the Archbishop suggested, might better be directed against poverty than against the poor.

Altschul parried this with a thrust of his own. "We have offered those people other places to live, and they refuse to go," he said. "Be careful, please, with such words as 'faith' and 'religious belief,' for what we often see is politics masquerading as religion, and, as we both know, the Holy Father, who is Pope to both of us, has been quite clear on this."

"I don't think he had in mind persecuting people for their beliefs," the Archbishop replied evenly.

Letting this pass, Altschul rose and went to the opposite end of the table, where a television set stood. As if he were a magician preparing to snatch away a veil and reveal a surprise, his voice became deep and dramatic. "Let me show you what does not help us," he intoned, "and, in fact, hinders us on the road to peace." He turned on the set with something of a flourish, and we watched a videotape of a caravan of Americans accompanying campesinos from the southern part of the country, who were returning with building materials to resettle their bombed-out villages. The delegation sat stony-faced, but Weakland had difficulty repressing a smile, for among the Americans were the faces of several Milwaukee Catholics.

That afternoon, at the American Embassy, Ambassador Walker echoed Altschul's call for patience. Walker joined the Foreign Service in 1961 and had since been posted to a series of Latin-American hot spots. Referring to President Cristiani as "Freddy"—as if the elected head of El Salvador were his faithful golden retriever—Walker told

the delegation that neither the right wing of the Salvadoran power élite (men like the ARENA's Roberto D'Au-
buisson, whom Walker described as a young Hitler) and
its supporters in the military nor the left (at least, as rep-
resented by the F.M.L.N.) should be allowed free rein.
Progress could be made only if the small but growing center could maintain its feeble grip on political power, he
said, and he noted that "the network of organizations"
supporting the F.M.L.N. was partly to blame for slowing
down the peace process and extending the war. Within
that suspect and shadowy network, of course, was the
SHARE Foundation, the group under whose auspices we
had come.

The meeting ended abruptly after the lights in the room
began to blink at short intervals and a public-address system directed all Embassy employees to leave for home by
four o'clock and to be off the streets by dark. Newspapers
being hawked on the streets featured photographs of
bloodied civilian casualties, a map indicating the main
combat areas, and headlines calling for the populace to
back the government. As daylight faded, we heard again
the sounds of low-flying helicopters. This time, we could
see them, as they criss-crossed the city just above the tops
of the tallest palm and eucalyptus trees.

We had hoped to hold our farewell dinner in another
of the good and very reasonably priced restaurants in the
capital, but because of the curfew the venue had to be
Centro Loyola. Before dinner, Archbishop Weakland and
Bishops Sullivan and Ramirez concelebrated the delegation's last Mass, in the center's chapel. At the front of the
chapel, directly behind the altar, is a wall of floor-to-ceiling
glass canted outward at the base and offering a panoramic

view of the city. The Mass started at six; ten minutes later, the first explosion was heard. A second, a third, a fourth mortar resonated dully within the chapel as the Archbishop read the words of the Gospel—Luke's story of Zacchaeus, who was so short that he had to climb a sycamore tree to see Christ passing by. An uneasy quiet fell as the Mass proceeded. Above the altar was a crucifix, and because of the way Christ's head was positioned He appeared to be looking down over San Salvador. Archbishop Weakland delivered a short homily, but I could recall no more of it than an allusion to the Church needing at times to climb the tree so that it, too, could get a better look at Christ. The bleeding figure on the cross silently imparted its own message that night.

On the way to the airport the next morning, we stopped off in the San Miguelito neighborhood, in the northern part of the capital, to visit Bishop Medardo Gómez, of the Lutheran Church in El Salvador. He was not at his office, and the delegation was instructed to go to a secret location, a few blocks away. There, in a private home with its window shades on the street side drawn, Bishop Gómez, a short, stocky fireplug of a man with a complexion and features indicating his Indian blood, apologized for inconveniencing the delegation because of his "personal situation." He had received a death threat—the latest of many—a few days earlier. But he did not dwell on that. He spoke instead about his pastoral work, and about the white wooden cross, seven feet high, that stood in the Resurrection Lutheran Church. It had been branded a "subversive cross" by the military, because Lutheran parishioners had inscribed the country's sins upon it: there was "Greed," and "Poverty," as there might be in any

country, but also "Torture," "Disappearances," "Bombings." The cross had been seized in a raid a year before,
but had recently been returned to the church. "I finally
understand why you Catholic clerics came up with the idea
of celibacy," Gómez told his visitors. "I have six children.
They wake up with nightmares. My wife is constantly worried. I could go through all of this, if it were only myself
I had to worry about. But I fear for them."

On an American Airlines plane bound for Miami, Archbishop Weakland leaned his head back on the headrest of the seat after finishing his breviary. I was sitting beside him. I had kept myself from taking his emotional pulse at each juncture of the trip, feeling that, while he had always been open with me, doing so would have been intrusive. Now I could word my question no better than "What went on there for you?"

He smiled over at me. "For one thing, I found out that I'm not a hero," he said, his tone betraying a certain wistful disappointment. "And I can't play a hero. I'm not moving to the slums. I'm not going back to work in El Salvador. But I know that I was jolted out of my provincialism—a silly provincialism that turns the fleeting issues back home into major concerns. I stood beside people who are on a blacklist—Rivera y Damas, Cortina, Gómez—and this is a blacklist that means they could be killed any day. My being on the Vatican's blacklist—what is that? It means even less than it did before. What risk do I really face? What could really be done to me?

"Martyrdom. That was a big part of this trip. I learned what martyrs are. I've been to all the sites in Rome; I've prayed at the tombs, knelt at the shrines; I've walked through the catacombs, the Circus Maximus, the Colosseum. But it never really touched me until I stood in Oscar Romero's room, at the altar where he was shot, at his tomb. The Jesuits' rooms—so simple, so ordinary. The place where they died—there are no candles dripping, no great shrine, just rosebushes. The graves of the Maryknoll sisters are no different from those of thousands of Salvadorans around them. I could never identify with our classic Catholic martyrs, but here I saw that martyrdom is not something you seek. A martyr, to me, is someone who just did his best and, because of circumstances, was killed. I'm sure the Salvadoran martyrs never thought of themselves as doing something special, something brave. No, they were working in the ordinariness of each day, looking at the events around them, reacting, trying to do—in some small, usually unnoticeable way—something they thought was right. When the moment of martyrdom came for the Jesuits, they were sleeping in their beds. Romero was saying Mass. The religious women were coming back from the airport. Doing ordinary things. I needed to realize the ordinariness of most of their lives, because, after all, that is what much of life is. What set these people apart is that they stood for a kind of religion—a religious belief—that influences lives. Religion, for them, was not a case of obeying rules but of influencing lives—and that is a very threatening thing to those who want to keep order. But if religion doesn't influence lives why bother with it?

"Only one Church will survive in Central America. Will it be the Church of Rivera y Damas and Romero, or will it be the Church of Cardinal Obando y Bravo? In the States, our Church doesn't face that kind of struggle for survival. Our struggle is more subtle, and therefore more insidious. We face being ignored. In a strange way, the trip was like a retreat for me—a time to get things into perspective, which is what my best retreats have given me. When you go to a place in which it is so difficult to hang on to one's faith and yet faith is so alive, what can you do but go back home and do whatever you can? Again, I am not a hero. I was afraid."

Weakland returned to Milwaukee on Thanksgiving, and the next morning he held a press conference. He had drafted a statement summarizing the group's activities in El Salvador, including the meeting with the F.M.L.N. But the Milwaukee press corps, which had been denied access to him for almost two weeks, was more interested in the details surrounding the denial of the Fribourg degree—an issue that had receded in the Archbishop's mind. In Washington, he had said that if he were a Catholic college president he would be a bit leery about speaking out. But now there was a different tone: he could not imagine keeping silent, he said, "unless you take out my tongue." The line made the national Associated Press wire, and the local papers gave it front-page play.

That Sunday, in his homily at the eight-o'clock Mass, the Archbishop discussed the three traits of a committed Christian. "Jesus promised those who followed his leadership only three things," he said. "They would be absurdly happy, entirely fearless, and always in trouble." He paused, as if to consider what he had just said. "Absurdly happy," he went on. "I am that. Entirely fearless—oh, boy, I have to work on that one a lot. Always in trouble." At this, the congregants burst into applause.

Boxes of letters, the vast majority voicing support over the Fribourg incident, had awaited the Archbishop in his office. A few more letters arrived early in the week, and after that the Archbishop thought the Fribourg matter was over with. But there was one more communication to come. At the end of the week, Weakland received a letter from the Vatican. Archbishop Pio Laghi, the head of the Vatican's Congregation for Catholic Education, wrote to say that the reason Weakland's name had not been cleared for the degree was that another congregation—Cardinal Ratzinger's Congregation for the Doctrine of the Faith— had not had sufficient time to evaluate the Archbishop's articles in the Catholic Herald on the "listening sessions" that the Archbishop had held on abortion. Weakland had in fact voluntarily sent the two articles to Rome—as he customarily does whenever something he has said or written might prompt letters to the Vatican—some months before, but he had received neither acknowledgment nor response. Archbishop Laghi's letter concluded, "I deeply regret the pain that you have suffered, I share it with you, and I sincerely assure you of my prayers so that the wound so inadvertently caused will be healed."

That the Vatican should offer an explanation of its actions was a rarity in itself; an apology was even rarer. But this was a private apology for what had mushroomed into a public deed. In his response, Weakland thanked Laghi for his "kind and gracious letter," but added, "Since most of the newspapers had been asking me if I had heard from you, I thought it might be wise to release your response. Not only does it clarify the situation but, I believe, also places the Vatican and yourself in a good light." When the story broke nationally and Laghi was asked by a reporter for the Religious News Service if indeed his letter was an apology, he shouted over the phone that it was simply "a clarification."

Whatever it may have been, Fribourg was over for the Archbishop. There were far more immediate and important matters on which he would have to deal with Vatican officials. One of his auxiliary bishops, Leo Brust, was reaching the mandatory retirement age of seventy-five, and the Archbishop wanted to make sure that his replacement was a man he could work with, and not the traditionalist he knew that the Vatican wanted as a countervailing force in Milwaukee. After two letters to the United States pronuncio, Archbishop Agostino Cacciavillan—the first was not answered to his satisfaction—Weakland elicited a guarantee that he would have veto power over the appointment. His second letter had been remarkably frank, informing the nuncio that the appointment of Robert Banks to Green Bay had not sat well, and that he and other American bishops felt "that it is totally useless to present names, and find it offensive that one is expected to go through a procedure that is a charade." He noted that many of his colleagues at the N.C.C.B. meeting "had hoped that the appointments of bishops would not continue to be controlled by Cardinal Law, Cardinal O'Connor, and Cardinal Krol; but it looks as if former procedures will still hold true."

The planned pastoral letter on the state of the priesthood in the archdiocese fell into place quickly after the El Salvador trip. The first twenty-two pages of the twenty-five-page document could have been written by almost any bishop in America: there was a shortage of priests, which would only get worse; priests were needed to preside over the sacraments; priests were overloaded; a growing number of parishes already had to do without pastors. But on page 23 the Archbishop broke new ground. If a congregation was without a resident priest and had no prospect of getting one in the near future, he wrote, "I would be willing to help the community surface a qualified candidate for ordained priesthood—even if a married man— and, without raising false expectations or unfounded hopes for him or the community, present such a candidate to the Pastor of the Universal Church for light and guidance."

This was scarcely a gentle lob into the Vatican's court. Weakland was saying that the Eucharist, not celibacy, was at the heart of the Church, and that he was ready to ordain a married man to the priesthood. Such an act was clearly in opposition to centuries of Church teaching and practice, and again Weakland was in newspapers across the country.

With the document finished and distributed to Milwaukee priests for their comments, Weakland went back to the business of being the leader of his archdiocese. The Little Eucharistic Lamb had taken to appearing in bright-red clothing at the eight-o'clock Mass at St. John's. After a psychologist whom the chancery consulted reported that this might presage an unpredictable mood swing, Weakland doubled the plainclothes guard around her at the Mass. On a more personal note, realizing that he would spend the rest of his ecclesiastical life in Milwaukee, the Archbishop decided that he wanted more privacy than his apartment in St. John's rectory afforded. He gave approval for the renovation of an old brick building on the grounds of the archdiocesan seminary; he moved in this spring.

And Briana Ziolkowski, from St. Philip Neri elementary school, came to dinner. She and two other winners of the Archbishop's art contest and their parents all sat down in the rectory dining room to a sumptuous meal of Sloppy

Joes encased in flaky French pastry and a dessert of fudge brownies à la mode. Briana wore a black-and-white striped dress and glistening patent-leather shoes. The Archbishop wore a plaid Pendleton over his clerical shirt, and soon unbuttoned his top button and pushed the Roman collar to the side. After the meal, he took his guests up to his suite of rooms and played the piano for an hour: Debussy, Chopin, Rachmaninoff. Often he will pander to popular taste and entertain with a little Scott Joplin, but that evening the Archbishop had decided to keep the concert "at a high level, befitting my guests."

AFTERWORD

I n the days and months after that evening with Briana Ziolkowski and the other art contest winners, the life, outlook, and daily work of Rembert Weakland of Milwaukee did not measurably change.

He traveled to Moscow and Siberia for an ecumenical meeting with leaders of the Russian Orthodox Church, newly enfranchised by the collapse of the Soviet Union, and later wrote a long article for *America* magazine warning the Catholic Church not to take advantage of the vacuum by aggressively proselytizing within the orthodox churches. Some Orthodox clergy had been implicated as secret KGB agents, and Catholic clergy had been exploiting this to win new members.

He also traveled to California to spend two winter weeks with his brother and sister. That spring, he moved into the newly renovated residence on the chancery grounds in Milwaukee.

Nationally, Weakland retained his standing and popularity among his fellow prelates. He was elected to the Bishops' Committee on Ecumenism and Interreligious Affairs, and to the planning committee that sets the agenda for the annual meeting.

But most of his time and efforts were concentrated in

his home archdiocese of Milwaukee. The continuing short-age of priests had necessitated parish mergers, making even more crucial an expanded training program for lay persons.

As for his dealings with the Vatican, nothing much changed there either. Weakland's draft proposal address-ing the priest shortage was sent to Rome and was consid-ered a matter of such explosive potential that it was presented to the Pope. The exchange of letters about that draft follows.

I include these letters in their entirety as much to explain the outcome of Weakland's bold act as to show what correspondence between a member of the American Catholic hierarchy and the Vatican reads like. Weakland's reply also, I think, provides an illuminating insight into a man who is—as he said in one of our conversations— "faithful to the Church while continually challenging it."

Regardless of the Vatican's objections to his proposal, Weakland published the document—revising it after he received comments and suggestions from within the arch-diocese, across America and around the world. It was called "Facing the Future with Hope: A Pastoral Letter on Parishes for the People of Milwaukee."

Archbishop Weakland sent the final version to the Vat-ican. As of this writing, he has not received a response. And, although his request has been in Rome for a year, he has not gotten a replacement for his auxiliary Leo Brust.

10 February 1991

Apostolic Nunciature
United States of America

Most Reverend Rembert G. Weakland, O.S.B.
Archbishop of Milwaukee
Milwaukee, Wisconsin

Dear Archbishop Weakland:

Archbishop Angelo Sodano, Pro-Secretary of State, has written me under date of January 30, 1991 regarding the first draft of your Pastoral Letter: "Facing the Future with Hope," which had been received at the Secretariat of State. Therein it was noted that, in examining the problem of the diminution of the number of priests in the Church, among other things a solution is proposed which arouses serious concerns, namely, the hypothesis of the ordination of married men.

After having duly informed the Holy Father, and upon his instruction, Archbishop Sodano asks me to communicate to you the following.

One cannot overlook the fact that, regarding the above-mentioned question, a clear indication in a quite different sense emerged in the general assembly of the Synod of Bishops last October.

Furthermore, as a result of the recent Synod, an appropriate Apostolic Exhortation is under preparation in which the Supreme Pontiff will offer the Universal Church orientations and directives to face adequately the same delicate question.

Keeping all this in mind, your intervention cannot but

appear to be out of place and, objectively, a sort of provocation.

I am sure you will appreciate these remarks and, as of now, I thank you for your consideration. No doubt, they are important also in view of the final text of your Pastoral Letter.

With cordial regards and best wishes, I remain
    Sincerely yours in Christ,

A. Cacciavillan
Apostolic Pro-Nuncio

April 24, 1991

Office of the Archbishop
Archdiocese of Milwaukee
Milwaukee Wisconsin

His Excellency
The Most Reverend Angelo Sodano
Pro-Secretary of State
Vatican City State, Europe

Your Excellency,

On February 10, 1991, I received a letter from His Excellency Archbishop Cacciavillan, in which he communicated to me the contents of a letter that you had written him concerning the first draft of the pastoral letter, "Facing the Future with Hope." The protocol number of the Apostolic Pro-Nuncio's letter was *2059/A*. I am appreciative of your concern and welcome the opportunity to write to you about the dialogue in my own diocese concerning the shortage of priests.

When we began our planning process throughout the diocese to deal with the reduction in the number of priests—it was in the Fall of 1989—I made it quite clear to the faithful and to the priests that the ordination of women and the ordination of married men could not be discussed as possible solutions. I am enclosing a letter I wrote to the priests in this regard, dated September 1, 1989, in which I explicitly mention that a discussion of such solutions would not be possible.

In a column in the diocesan newspaper, dated October

19, 1989, I reiterated the same idea to all the faithful.

My own experience with regard to what happened in the various regions of the diocese might be of some help to you. The results of my saying that these solutions could not be discussed were anything but positive. Region after region of the Archdiocese — even the more reserved — protested that they were not permitted to examine *all* the solutions. In particular, they adduced many reasons for their desire to discuss the ordination of married men.

They remarked, for example, that the admission of married Episcopal clergy into the Roman Catholic priesthood has been accepted and even goes under the name of "the pastoral solution." They alluded to the strong pressures from the Protestant tradition, with the erosion of our own Catholic identity, if we were reduced to a Liturgy of the Word for any length of time. In a country such as the United States in which that Protestant tradition based on the Liturgy of the Word is so strong, this fear is not unfounded. They also point out the enormous expenditures and efforts made in the last decade for vocations with only a small result. They point out the large number of exceptionally good candidates who decide not to enter the priesthood, not because they have no regard for the celibate commitment, but because they value it so highly and do not want to run the risk of breaking it. Naturally, other reasons are adduced, as well.

Therefore, my response in the first draft of the pastoral letter was simply a way of letting people know that I had listened to their fears and was not turning a deaf ear to them. I did this in the most respectful way I knew how. You can well understand that in today's world to tell people that they are forbidden to discuss something usually brings about unhappy results. I relate this experience knowing how typical it is and hope it can be of some help to you.

I had not seen that this subject was really thoroughly debated at the recent Synod. I was under the impression that it had been excluded from the discussion. Perhaps this was wrongly reported in the U.S. press.

One consoling thought, however, emerged from all of this discussion in the Archdiocese and the U.S. in general. In the post-Council II period we have indeed catechized our people well about the role of the Mass in our Catholic tradition and the fact that we are a Eucharistic people. This is so tied in to our Catholic identity that no halfway solutions seem acceptable.

My correspondence as a result of this first draft has been enormous from all over the world. I was also surprised how many bishops have written to me and commented favorably on the draft. I suspect that this is a sign of a desire for a deeper discussion on the issues involved. I am sure the Holy Father has considered all of these questions in summarizing his own response to the last Synod.

As you can see from the documents enclosed and from the wording of the first draft itself, it is not and never would be my intention to do anything not approved by the Holy Father or not in accord with the practice of the Universal Church.

Thank you for this opportunity to respond.

Sincerely yours in the Lord,

Most Reverend Rembert G. Weakland, O.S.B.
Archbishop of Milwaukee